Bagels, Bialys, Pizza, and Pie

Bagels, Bialys, Pizza, and Pie:

A Collection of

Reasonably Healthy, Mostly Vegetarian

Family Favorites

from the

Quotidian

to the

Extraordinary

Hy Ginsberg

©2020 Hy Ginsberg

All rights reserved.

All photographs (and most of the pottery…) by the author.

ISBN: 978-1-7352573-0-3
Library of Congress Control Number: 2020911429

First edition.

Least Obeisance Publishing
Shrewsbury, Massachusetts

www.leastobeisance.com

For my kids, Evan and Daisy, who inspired this project.

And for those other "kids" (all grown now), for whom I've had the pleasure of cooking now and then over the past couple of decades: Kayleigh, Rachel, Samantha, Ben, Nellie, Emma, Becky, Sam, and Jake – I hope (and suspect) that you will each find a favorite recipe or two somewhere herein.

And for my wife, Anne, *of course*.

And for *me*.

(I'm really quite pleased *you* have a copy, too.)

Contents

Introduction	1
Preliminary Notes	3
On Measuring	3
Ovens!	3
Ingredients	4
Hy's Pies	5
Half and Half Pie Crust	6
Bing Cherry Pie	8
Peach Pie	10
Pumpkin Pie	12
Pecan Pie	14
Chocolate Pudding Pie with a Walnut Crust	16
Other Desserts	19
Baklava	21
Candied Cherries	25
Sicilian Almond Cookies	27
Lemon Raspberry Cookies	28
Hermit Cookies	30
Tahini Sandwich Cookies	33
Mandel Bread	34
Lemon Bars	37
Rugelach	38
Angel Food Cake	40
Chocolate Bread	42
Cinnamon Buns	44
Chocolate Cake	46
Orange Cake	48
Ice Cream Sandwiches	50
Date Balls	52
Nut Balls	53
Vanilla or Chocolate Pudding	54
Indian Pudding	56

Rice Pudding 58
Tapioca Pudding 60

Breakfast 63

Granola 64
Chocolate Granola 66
Pancakes 69
Waffles 71
Dutch Baby Pancake 72

Salads, Snacks, Sauces, Spreads, Etc. 73

Caesar Salad 74
Sour Garlic Pickles 76
Vietnamese Cucumber Salad 78
Candied Nuts 79
Marmalade 80
Modica 82
Peanut Sauce 83
Tahini Yogurt Sauce 84
Cucumber Yogurt Sauce 84
Surfer Spread 85
Mint Julep 86

Quickbread 89

Drop Biscuits 90
Strawberry Muffins 92
Blueberry Muffins 93
Pumpkin Chocolate Chip Muffins 96
Corn Bread 98
Irish Soda Bread 100
Date Nut Bread 102
Banana Chocolate Chip Scones 104

Bread 107

General Instructions 108
Challah 110
      6-Strand Braid 112
Bagels 113
Bagel Crackers 116
Bialys 118
Khachapuri Rolls 121
Dinner or Burger Rolls 124
French Bread Baguettes 127
Hy's Best Sandwich Bread 129

Sunflower Bread	132
Fruit, Nut, and Seed Bread	134
Oat Bread	136
Potato Bread	138
Pita Bread	140
Flour Tortillas	142
Breadsticks	144
Breadcrumbs	146

Pizza — 147

General Notes	148
Pizza Dough	151
Pizza Sauce	153
New York Style Pizza	154
Vegetarian Sausage	155
Sicilian Pizza	156
"Dancing Heart" Pizza	158
Macaroni and Cheese Pizza	159
Potato Pizza	160
Old Bay Pizza	162
Scallion Pancake Pizza	164
Grilled Pizza	166
Focaccia	168
Focaccia with Leeks	170
Herbed Flatbread	173

Soup — 175

Simple But Excellent Carrot Soup	176
African Peanut Soup	178
Potato Cheese Soup	180
Seafood Soup	182
Vegetable Stock	184

Dinner — 185

Cheddar Ale Sauce	186
Broccoli Ring	188
Cashew Burgers	192
Gyro Pockets	194
Fake Chicken with Cashews	197
Fake Chicken	199
Crab Cakes	200
Cold Sesame Noodles	202
Pasta with Crispy Chickpeas	205
Garlic Pasta	207

Macaroni and Cheese 208
Spinach Ravioli 211
Pasta with Roasted Cauliflower 213
Spinach Calzone 215
Black Tofu 217
Roasted Tofu 220
Potatonik 223
Mashed Potato Casserole 225
Vegetarian Pastelón 226
Saag Paneer 228
Shrimp Etouffee 231
    Shrimp Stock 232
    Creole Seasoning 232
Mujadara 233
Turkish Pizza 235
Vegetable Fried Rice 237
Saffron Rice Pilaf 240
Varenikas 243
Vegetable Pot Pies 245
Nothing and Like It 247

Appendices   249
  Recommended Reading 249
  Calculating Nutritional Information 250

Index   253

Introduction

I don't expect anybody to buy this book – it's a $35 paperback by someone with questionable qualifications. (Here they are: I've been cooking – and especially baking – for 40 years, and for the past 20 have generally been in charge of dinner for my family. That's mostly it. I am pretty good at it, though, and there are a lot of *really* good things to cook in here… Also, I grew up in New York, so I know what a decent bagel should taste like – ditto for bialys and pizza.) No, if you have this book, then I strongly suspect that I gave it to you. (If you did buy it, great and thank you. You should know that I'm not raking it in – I make exactly $1 for every copy sold. This is not a brilliant money making scheme on my part…)

So if I don't expect to sell any – or many, anyway – why did I go to such considerable trouble putting together such a damn nice book (if I do say so myself – I am quite proud of it…)? To put it simply, for my children. One day they will want to know how to make the things I've been cooking for them all these years, and – life being what it is – I can't promise to be there to teach them. (At present they are perfectly happy to let me do the cooking…)

That, at least, was my original motivation. Then I started finding it convenient to have all my recipes in one place, and it became a book for *me*. But when I started adding photographs, and it started to look so very *good*, well, my friends, that's when my delusions of grandeur began, and I started to think that *everyone* should have a copy. And so here it is, available to everyone, even if no one buys it… If you are reading the preview online, and not actually holding a copy in your hands, then it's yours if you can get past the ludicrous price… As I said at the start, I don't expect you to. It's ridiculous. Best I could do, though, and I would love for you to have one. And I think you'll be pleased if you do…

As for the recipes, they are, as I could not resist mentioning in the title, mostly vegetarian (there are a few seafood dishes), and reasonably healthy. I avoid butter where I don't find it necessary (and most of my cookie and cake recipes have none), but include it where I think it makes a difference. There is no cream – heavy or light – in anything. Plenty of vegetables. A few good things to do with tofu (really).

You will find a number of healthy and delicious meat alternatives. Bagels, bialys, pizza, and pie, *of course* (and not just any recipes for these pinnacles of culinary achievement – the *best* recipes – I *worked* on them, in most cases for *years*…), but also a host of other fine foods, from pancakes and drop biscuits (the quotidian) to baklava and etouffee (the extraordinary). Lots of breads. *Puddings*.

I put dessert first because – as alluded to in my second paragraph – life is short. And for the same compelling reason, I strongly recommend making the chocolate bread *immediately*.

Happy cooking.

-Hy

P.S. Recipes evolve; this cookbook – like all others – is a snapshot in time, portraying what I currently believe to be the best versions of all its contents. But just because I have finally committed it to print and sent it off to be published doesn't mean I won't continue to fiddle, and if you'd like to keep abreast of any changes, corrections, or improvements, check in from time to time at *www.leastobeisance.com*. Perhaps I will even post a new recipe there occasionally.

Preliminary Notes

On Measuring

I have three sets of measuring cups. When I measure and then weigh a cup of flour I get 134 grams, 118 grams, and 137 grams (plus or minus about 2 grams, repeating the process a few times). According to *King Arthur*, whose flour I am weighing (so they should know), a cup of flour weighs 120 grams. So one of my measuring cups is pretty close; the other two are *way off*. If I'm measuring 7 cups of flour for a bread, for example, then the worst of my three measuring cups is off by $7 \times 17 = 119$ grams – just a gram short of *a full cup*. That's crazy.

What's the point? *You can't trust your measuring cups.* If you want consistent, reliable results, then you have to weigh your ingredients.

(But can you trust your scale? I think you can. At least, I have three scales, and they all agree pretty much exactly.)

Ovens!

We bought a top-of-the-line, name-brand oven. (Okay, it's a *GE*.) Oh, how I hate it…

It *doesn't keep the temperature constant*. If you shut it off while you're baking, and then immediately restart it at the same temperature, it will very often report that in fact the temperature is *40 or 50 degrees cooler* than it's set for, and go into its "preheat" cycle. (If the temperature is so much cooler, *and it knows it*, why does it need me to prompt it to get hotter?)

It seems to do a little better when using convection, and for that reason you'll see that I specify the use of convection in a lot of my recipes. This is mostly there as a reminder to myself, so I don't have to think about it each time. Occasionally, if I think it is important, I will explicitly recommend *against* using convection, but again, this is just a matter of what seems to work best with my oven. Your oven will no doubt work differently, and you may have to make adjustments. On the other hand if mine was perfect and yours less so, you'd have to adjust for that as well, and ultimately it seems to me that baking times and temperatures can't be followed blindly, at least not at our current stage of technology. Maybe one day.

Another thing: Conventional wisdom says to set your oven 25° cooler when using convection, but my oven *makes that adjustment automatically* – in other words, when I set it for 350° with convection, it actually heats to 325°. I suspect most modern ovens do the same. What about yours? Check - set your oven to 350° with convection, and as soon as it reaches temperature, shut it off, and immediately (and without opening it) set it to 350° *without* convection. If it reports that it's at 325°, it's making the adjustment, just like mine. If not, then when you follow recipes that specifically call for convection (in this book and elsewhere), lower the temperature by 25°.

Ingredients

Butter: The recipes assume that the butter you're using is unsalted; if you use salted butter, adjust accordingly.

Eggs: First of all, "large" is a euphemism for small, and second, you'll never convince me that all of the eggs in any given carton are really the same size. So this is pretty much where all pretenses at precise measurement fall apart. Oh well. Where it really matters I've specified the amount by volume or weight, instead of just by a number of eggs. For what it's worth I usually use eggs that are called "extra large" (i.e. not all that small…).

Flour: The recipes were all tested with *King Arthur* flours (*All Purpose Flour*, or, when specified, *Bread Flour*). It might matter, especially in breads – different brands have different amounts of protein (due to the varieties of wheat used), and in particular different concentrations of gluten. If you use a different brand of flour, you might need to make adjustments (either to the amount of flour or the amount of liquid).

Milk: I use lowfat (1%) milk; use whatever you have around, it will be fine.

Oil: By "oil" I always mean vegetable oil, pretty much any kind except olive oil – I explicitly call for olive oil when that's what I intend. Unless it's organic, I avoid canola oil, because, although it's purportedly the healthiest, rumor has it that they go very heavy on the pesticides. For conventionally grown oils I stick with safflower or sunflower, which are both supposed to be very healthy. (My understanding of the relative nutritional properties of various oils stems from some reading I did decades ago; don't take my word for it, look into it yourself.) Coconut oil, which enjoyed a great deal of popularity in the recent past, is probably the worst possible choice from a health perspective; I never use it (but again, what do I know).

In the rare instances where I fry with any appreciable quantity of oil (such as frying tofu or potatoes in "1/4 inch" or so), I go with whatever comes cheaply in a giant container (most of it gets discarded afterwards anyway).

Salt: This means *table salt* (preferably iodized, unless you are sure you get enough iodine in your diet); finely granulated sea salt can be substituted, but if you use kosher salt, then you can't measure by volume – kosher salt is less dense (at least partly due to the larger size grains), and – to make it even more complicated – different brands have vastly different densities. (If you're measuring by weight, then it's the same for any type of salt.)

Yeast: I always use "active dry" yeast in my recipes, for the simple reason that when I started baking bread in the 1970's, "instant" yeast hadn't yet been invented. And since active dry yeast and I have always gotten along fine, I haven't bothered to switch. If you're an instant yeast enthusiast, I'm sure you can make the recipes work with what you've got.

Hy's Pies

Half and Half Pie Crust
Adapted from "Tassajara Cooking" by Edward Espe Brown.

Half white flour and half whole wheat pastry flour, half butter and half oil; this is both the healthiest and the tastiest pie crust around.

Yield: 2 9-inch crusts (for one two-crust pie or two one-crust pies).

> 150 g flour (1 1/4 C)
> 150 g whole wheat pastry flour (1 1/4 C)
> 1/4 tsp salt
> 1/3 C oil
> 1/3 C butter
> 5–6 Tbs ice water

Combine the dry ingredients, and mix in the oil. Cut in the butter until it's reduced to pea-sized pieces. Then add the water, a tablespoon at a time, until the dough holds together well. (Don't be tempted to stop at less than 5 tablespoons – it's not ready, and will be impossible to work with.)

Form the dough into a ball, divide in half, and roll out on a well floured surface.

To transfer the rolled out crust into a pie tin (or onto a pie), lay the rolling pin on the crust near one edge, lift the crust onto the rolling pin (using a "dough knife" or "bench scraper" or "dough scraper" – there doesn't seem to be an agreed upon name for this simple and essential tool), and slowly and carefully roll it up. Then lift the pin to the pie and unroll the crust into place.

Use a scissor to trim the crust(s) to about 1/2 inch past the edge of the pie tin, then crimp the edges. If there's a top crust, cut a few slits to let steam escape.

Notes:

> Tears or holes in the crust are easily repaired: cement a small piece from the edge (or from the last trimmed crust) into place with a little bit of the ice water, and press it flat with your fingers.
>
> On the one hand, the bottom of a two-crust pie is a bit larger than the top, which would suggest dividing the dough in "half" somewhat unevenly and allocating the larger piece to the bottom. On the other, the top crust is the one that's on display, and the thinner you have to roll it, the more likely it is to tear. (And once it's on the pie, repairs tend to be awkward and noticeable.) I compromise by dividing more or less in half, and if there is a "half" that seems a little larger, I use it for the bottom.

Also for a two-crust pie, wait until the top crust is ready and rolled up on the rolling pin before filling the bottom crust – that way there's no time for the bottom crust to get soggy.

To keep the dough from sticking to the counter, it helps to flip it over once (use the dough knife), when it's about 6 or 7 inches in diameter, and add more flour underneath.

"Pea-sized" is really and truly what you are aiming for, in terms of the size of the butter pieces – if you are overambitious and cut it more finely, you will end up with a dough that is harder to work with, and the same will happen if you leave the pieces too large.

Although you can cut in the butter between two knives, scissor style, the "pastry cutter" is really one of the finest inventions ever (thank you Elmer L. Dennis, who called it a "dough blender" in his 1927 patent). You need one.

For a one-crust pie it is sometimes beneficial to partially prebake the crust: poke some holes in the bottom and sides with a fork (to keep it from puffing up), and bake at 375° for 5 – 10 minutes (see photo below).

I usually use convection when baking my pies, but they are fine without it (without convection the actual temperature is somewhat higher – see page 3 – so they might finish cooking on the earlier side of the time range).

Bing Cherry Pie

The best cherry pie you ever had, by far.

(If you think you don't like cherry pie, then you've probably only ever had the usual, horrible, sickeningly sweet version that starts with sour cherries and then overcompensates with a boatload of sugar. Stores around here don't even sell sour cherries, so that has never been an option for me, but this version, with bing cherries, is an entirely different creation. Give it a try; you won't be disappointed.)

> 2 lbs bing cherries, pitted (fresh if possible, but frozen will do)
> 250 g sugar (1 1/4 C)
> 6 Tbs granulated ("minute") tapioca (57 g)
> 3 Tbs fresh lemon juice (about 1 lemon)
>
> 2 pie crusts (page 6)

Mix together all the filling ingredients, and stir them every now and then while you make the crusts. (If the cherries are frozen, make sure they have some time to defrost before the pie goes in the oven.)

Just before you are ready to roll out the bottom crust, preheat the oven to 425°, with convection, with a shelf in the middle or just above.

Assemble the pie, waiting to fill the bottom crust until the top crust is ready (trim and crimp the edges, cut slits in the top). Bake for 15 minutes at 425°, then turn the oven down to 375° and bake for another 25 – 35 minutes, until the filling begins to boil out of the slits in the top.

Serve at room temperature.

Notes:

> The amount of tapioca has been carefully chosen to give a pie that is moist but still holds together well at room temperature. If you prefer to serve it warm, increase the tapioca somewhat (or the pie will be runny). How much? I don't know – I like my pie at room temperature… And it depends on how warm it is. Similarly, if you intend to serve it cold, decrease the tapioca somewhat, or the pie will be stiff and a little dry.

> "Minute" tapioca is ground into small bits that contribute a barely noticeable, soft, chewiness to the filling. It is undoubtedly possible to adapt the recipe to use tapioca flour (which, when I started making pies was unheard of – now, as an essential ingredient in gluten-free baking, it is ubiquitous). I don't because I like the texture, but feel free to experiment, if you are so inclined…

Peach Pie

If you have good peaches that are truly ripe – juicy, sweet, and delicious – then peach pie is *heavenly*, and really can't be beat.

    2 1/2 lbs ripe peaches
    215 g sugar (about 1 C plus 1 Tbs)
    1/4 C granulated ("minute") tapioca (38 g)
    juice of 1/2 lemon
    pinch salt

    2 pie crusts (page 6)

    1 egg
    1 Tbs milk
    turbinado sugar

Begin by making the filling (it benefits from some time to steep while you make the crust – the sugar brings out the juice from the peaches, which softens up the tapioca a bit). Peel and slice the peaches, then mix with the remaining filling ingredients (the egg, milk, and turbinado sugar are for the topping).

Next make the crust. Once you have the bottom crust laid out in the pie tin, preheat the oven to 425°, with convection, with a rack in the middle or just above.

Peach pie is traditionally given a woven lattice crust, which can be a little tricky. It helps to roll out the top crust, transfer it to a floured cookie sheet, and put it in the freezer for 15 minutes before weaving. When it's ready, pour the filling into the bottom crust, then slice the top crust into inch-wide strips (with a fluted pastry cutter if you have one). Weave these gently over the pie. (There is no way around it, this is going to entail lifting some of the strips and bending them back to sneak perpendicular strips under them; it can be done – have faith; be careful.) Trim and crimp the edges as usual, then mix together the egg and milk, brush the crust, and sprinkle with turbinado sugar.

Bake for 15 minutes, then lower the temperature to 375° and continue to bake for 20 – 30 minutes, until the crust is nicely browned and the filling is bubbling.

Serve at room temperature.

Notes:

    Buy extra peaches! They will not all ripen simultaneously, and by the time most of them are ready, a couple are bound to be past.

    The discussion of tapioca at the end of the cherry pie recipe (see page 8) applies equally here; take a look…

Pumpkin Pie

Delicious and nutritious – the perfect food.

    1/2 C sugar
    1/2 tsp salt
    2 tsps cinnamon
    1/2 tsp ginger
    1/4 tsp nutmeg
    1/4 tsp cloves
    1 15 oz. can pumpkin
    1 egg, beaten
    1 1/2 C milk
    1 Tbs molasses

    1 partially baked pie crust (page 6)

Preheat the oven to 450°, with convection, with a rack in the middle or just below.

Mix together the dry ingredients, then add the rest of the ingredients and mix until smooth. Pour into the partially baked pie crust.

Bake for 15 minutes, then lower the oven temperature to 350° and continue baking for an additional 40 minutes, or until set.

Notes:

    I beat the eggs in the empty pumpkin can, then pour the milk through it to help liberate every last bit of pumpkin.

    The amount of filling is dictated by the size of a can of pumpkin, but if you're feeling bold and ambitious, most pie crusts can handle about 25% more (I say "most" because it turns out – *amazingly* – that not every 9 inch pie tin is the same). Certainly if you happen to be making four pies, you should consider using five times the filling.

    Personally, I like my pumpkin pie chilled, but there are those who prefer it at room temperature. I encourage you to accommodate everyone – make (at least) two…

Pecan Pie

There's no getting around it, it's pecan pie, so it's *sweet*. But it's not *please-take-me-to-the-hospital, I-think-I'm-going-to-die* sweet, like most other pecan pies. I have also increased the quantity of pecans well above the norm, and the result is a pie that is comparatively healthy, *edible* – which is impressive for a pecan pie – and especially delicious.

    1/4 C sugar
    2 Tbs flour
    1/4 tsp salt
    1 C light corn syrup
    2 eggs
    1 tsp vanilla
    2 C pecans (230 g)

    1 partially baked pie crust (page 6)

Preheat the oven to 375°, with convection, with a rack just below the middle.

Mix the sugar, flour, and salt in a small mixing bowl. Add the corn syrup, eggs, and vanilla, and whisk until smooth. Spread the pecans in the partially baked pie crust, and pour the filling mixture evenly over the nuts. Bake for 35 – 40 minutes, until nicely browned on top.

Note: I'm sure a raw pie crust would work fine, but if you make the crust before you start on the filling (and why wouldn't you), and you have the oven preheating anyway (which, again, why wouldn't you), then you may as well partially prebake the pie crust.

Chocolate Pudding Pie with a Walnut Crust

Amazing. The directions below are for the crust; make the crust first, then make the pudding (page 54), pour the pudding into the crust, and refrigerate. (The pudding recipe makes a little more than will fit in the pie; fill a couple of small bowls with the remainder.)

    7 oz walnuts
    3 Tbs sugar
    2 Tbs butter
    1/4 C flour
    1/4 tsp salt
    2 tsps water

    1 batch of chocolate pudding (page 54)

Preheat the oven to 350°, without convection, with a rack in the middle or just above. Line the bottom of 9 inch pie pan with parchment paper (grease the bottom lightly first to keep the parchment paper in place), and butter the sides of the pan generously.

Blend everything except the water in a food processor until the walnuts are very finely chopped, then add the water and process briefly until it comes together into a dough. Press the dough into the pie pan with your fingers, working it up the sides, until it conforms to the shape of the pan. Bake for 15 – 20 minutes, until richly browned.

Notes:

    The recipe has been carefully crafted to resist slumping down the sides while still browning nicely, but it is a delicate balance – if it does happen to slump some, build it back up with the back of a spoon as soon as it comes out of the oven.

    If you must use convection, you might have to increase the temperature or the cooking time to get the crust to brown properly.

    Store your walnuts in the freezer! They go rancid very quickly at room temperature. (The refrigerator will suffice if your freezer is full.)

    Some people like whipped cream…

Other Desserts

Baklava

The epitome of Middle Eastern desserts: sheets of phyllo dough, filled with chopped nuts, soaked in sweet syrup. Ideally, the syrup permeates the pastry without also making it soggy – it should retain a bit of a pleasant crunch. It is a delicate balance. The good news is that, even if perfection is elusive, extreme excellence – which is close enough – is absolutely attainable, and in any case imperfect baklava remains a heavenly confection – you will receive no complaints.

The mix of nuts is a matter of personal preference; I am partial to a combination of almonds and pistachios, or almonds, pistachios, and walnuts. I do not disparage the use of pistachios or walnuts exclusively, but for some reason I cannot explain the use of almonds on their own strikes me as a mistake. If you happen to choose to use only walnuts (which is certainly how I first tasted it), consider adding a bit of cinnamon.

And then there's the elephant in the recipe: phyllo dough. Infamous, the stuff of nightmares… Sometimes it will go so well that you will wonder what all the fuss is about (pray for beginners' luck the first time you use it); other times it will live up to its reputation for obstinacy and ill will – the sheets will stick together inseparably, crack in long lines down the middle, or just randomly tear. Here is the best advice I can muster:

> Defrost your phyllo dough in the refrigerator overnight – although it is possible to defrost it quickly (an hour or two on the counter), it's risky.
>
> Make sure it's reasonably fresh – if you bought the phyllo dough six months ago and have had it in the freezer ever since, it *might* still be okay, but then again it might not.
>
> As you work with it, the phyllo will quickly dry out, so work with only some of it at a time – keep what you can wrapped in its original plastic bag, and keep the rest under a sheet of aluminum foil with a *lightly* dampened dish towel over it (the towel is primarily there to hold down the foil, and must not touch the phyllo dough at all – it will glue it together if it does…).

And finally, the butter. Each sheet will be brushed with a thin layer of butter, and there is no way around it, that adds up to a lot of butter. Everywhere else in this book I go out of my way to minimize the use of butter; with phyllo dough, I don't fight it. How much baklava are you going to eat anyway? – a few pieces. It's okay. There are those who claim you can use oil, or a combination of butter and oil, and maybe they are right; I haven't tried.

In any case, in the butter lies the key: If you want to make a baklava that is both syrupy and crisp, *you have to "clarify" the butter.* Butter has a good deal of water in it (and a higher percentage in the U.S. than in Europe), and when working with a lot of butter and phyllo dough, *you will notice* – you melt a stick of butter, brush each sheet lightly, and when you get down towards the last of the butter, it will be distinctly watery. At that point you are brushing water onto your phyllo, which is certainly not going to help keep it crisp. (You can cheat: Melt your butter, and when it starts to get watery, throw it out it and start over with a fresh stick. That works well enough, and as I mentioned earlier no one will complain, but it is ultimately unsatisfying – your baklava will not be as crisp as it could be, unless you compensate by skimping on the syrup, in which case it will not be as syrupy as it could be…) Clarifying the butter removes the water (as well as the milk solids), and is not difficult to do. Here is the technique: Melt two sticks over a very low heat. Eventually, they will start to sputter and pop – this is the water, which sinks to the bottom, boiling off. Leave it alone until the sputtering slows and eventually more or less ceases; at this point all that is left is butterfat and milk solids. Some of the solids will have floated to the top; gently skim these off with a slotted spoon. The rest will have sunk to the bottom and browned; pour the liquid through a couple of layers of cheese cloth to remove these. Done. (In theory it no longer needs refrigeration; if I am not using mine right away, I refrigerate it anyway – preferably in the small saucepan I will use to melt it for my baklava.) Two sticks makes more clarified butter than you will really need, but it keeps very well, and you can use it for any future frying needs.

At the risk of never getting to the actual recipe, I will add one more introductory note: There is a great historical debate over whether one should pour cold syrup over hot baklava, or hot syrup over cold baklava (apparently, all are agreed that they must be of opposite temperatures); I fall into the first camp but only because that's what I first tried, and I'm very pleased with the results. Feel free to experiment and form your own opinion.

Syrup:

    3/4 C water
    250 g sugar (1 1/4 C)
    1/4 C honey
    1 Tbs fresh lemon juice
    1 Tbs rose water (or orange blossom water)

Filling:

    1 lb finely chopped nuts (about 3 – 3 1/2 cups after chopping)
    1/3 C sugar

    Optional: If using all walnuts, 1 tsp cinnamon

Phyllo:

    1 lb phyllo dough
    2 sticks of butter (you will not use all of it…)

First make the syrup – combine all of the syrup ingredients except the rose water in a saucepan, bring to a boil, and simmer vigorously (boil gently?) for 10 minutes. Add the rose water and cook for another half minute or so, then refrigerate. (I leave mine uncovered, so that it cools more quickly and doesn't accumulate any extra liquid through condensation.)

One pound of phyllo dough should contain about 40 reasonably sized sheets, or maybe 20 large sheets that you will need to cut in half – check your package to confirm. Ideally, we will use 10 sheets on the bottom, 10 on the top, and then five layers of 4 sheets each in between – 40 sheets total. (If your count is slightly different, adjust accordingly.) This provides for six layers of filling, so each layer will have about 1/2 cup of chopped nuts, rounded up a bit.

Melt your clarified butter (or a single, unmodified stick if you are choosing that route, in which case you will start over with a new stick when you deem it appropriate).

Lightly grease a 9 × 13 × 2 inch baking tray, or something similar. I use glass; since you are eventually going to pour cold syrup into the hot pan, if you do use glass, make sure it is a type (such as "pyrex") made to withstand such thermal inconsistencies; otherwise use metal. With a sharp knife, trim some of the phyllo to a size just a bit larger than the bottom of the pan (if your pan tapers up, then the sheets used towards the top will be slightly larger). As described above, try to keep the phyllo from drying out as you work with it. Carefully remove one sheet of phyllo, lay it flat on the counter, brush it lightly with butter, and place it in the pan. Some imperfection in placement is okay and even desirable – little wrinkles and misalignments add to the structure of the final product. Repeat, until you have ten sheets forming the bottom of the pastry, then sprinkle evenly with a little more than 1/2 cup of the nut mixture.

Continue to form the middle layers: trim the phyllo as needed, lightly brush a sheet with butter, lay it over the nut mixture, and repeat with three more sheets – the middle layers are 4 sheets thick. Sprinkle with another slightly rounded 1/2 cup of nuts, and then do it all again…

At some appropriate time during the process, preheat the oven to 350°, without convection, with a rack in the middle or just above.

On top of the fifth 4-sheet layer, sprinkle whatever remains of the nut mixture – it should be about the same as the other layers. Then top with the remaining ten sheets of phyllo (each dutifully brushed with butter, of course). If you are a sheet or two short or over, no worries – the box might not have had precisely 40, or perhaps you miscounted somewhere (counting to 10 and then to 4 over and over is in some ways the hardest part of this recipe – you think I'm joking, but just wait…).

Use a sharp paring knife to carefully slice the baklava into diamonds. Ideally you want to cut through all the layers *but not the bottom* – try to leave the bottom (ten sheets) intact. It is of course impossible to do this precisely, so just do the best you can.

Bake the baklava for 30-35 minutes, until it is golden brown.

As soon as the baklava comes out of the oven, slowly and carefully pour the chilled syrup along the lines you cut into the top, as well as along the very edges – the idea is to get the syrup to seep into and saturate the baklava, while avoiding pouring it directly onto the top layers of phyllo as much as possible (it's not possible to do it perfectly, of course, which is fine and even good – some syrup on top is expected – you just don't want to soak the whole surface).

Allow to fully cool – and preferably to "steep" overnight – before serving.

Notes:

For the record, this is about 3/4 of the syrup called for in most traditional baklava recipes. It's still plenty sweet and syrupy, but if you want to scale up a bit, give it a try. (I suggest restraint, though – scaling all the way up to a full cup of water yields an unpleasantly soggy baklava. Not that we didn't eat it anyway…)

If your phyllo dough proves uncooperative, you can use torn sheets in the middle layers – piece them together the best you can; no one will notice. Try to preserve a pristine sheet or two for the top, where it's most visible.

Although it is customary to trim all the phyllo to more or less fit the pan, there are proponents for letting it go "wild" over the edges – that yields some extra crunchy phyllo goodness to the edge and corner pieces. You can do this starting with the bottom sheets, draping them up over the edges, or just let the sheets grow larger as you move up.

If you are using more than one variety of nut, it is prudent to grind them separately – walnuts grind more quickly than almonds, for example.

Candied Cherries
Adapted from www.fromthelarder.co.uk.

The quantities below are for a pound of cherries; seeing as the process takes about *2 1/2 weeks*, it makes sense to make considerably more – aside from the pitting, it's the same amount of work.

I use bing cherries because that's what's easily available, but if you have sour cherries, fine – they end up plenty sweet.

    1 lb cherries, pitted
    500 ml boiling water
    600 g sugar, in total

Day 1: Put the cherries in a saucepan, pour the boiling water over them, and cook for 5 minutes. (Don't worry if they don't boil, but if they do, turn them down to a simmer.) Drain the cherries, reserving 340 ml of the liquid. Set the cherries aside in a heat-proof container. Return the reserved liquid to the saucepan, add 200g sugar, stir, and bring to a boil. Pour the syrup over the cherries, cover the container, and leave at room temperature overnight.

Day 2: Strain the syrup into a saucepan and return the cherries to the container. Add 48g of sugar to the syrup, stir, bring to a boil, and simmer for 2 or 3 minutes. Pour the syrup back over the cherries, cover, and let soak.

Days 3 – 7: Repeat the process from Day 2.

Day 8: Strain the syrup into a saucepan, add 68g of sugar, stir, and heat gently. When the sugar has completely dissolved, add the cherries to the saucepan, and bring to a boil. Simmer for 2 or 3 minutes, then return the cherries and syrup to the container, cover, and leave for two days.

Day 10: Repeat the process from Day 8, but with only 44g of sugar. Leave the cherries in their covered contained for four days.

Day 14: Drain the cherries (reserve the syrup for drinks…). Spread them on wire racks in a warm, dry place to dry for two or three days, until they are no longer sticky. If necessary they can be finished in a cooling oven.

Store in an airtight container.

Note: As long as they are well dried, these last well over a year frozen, refrigerated, or at room temperature.

Sicilian Almond Cookies

These cookies are the reason you go to all the trouble of candying a vast quantity of cherries every summer (see the recipe on the preceding page). But in case you were not so industrious, any and all of the optional toppings make delicious and impressive cookies (see the photo before the Table of Contents).

Yield: About 24 cookies.

>336 g blanched almonds
>224 g sugar
>60 g egg whites (from about 2 eggs)
>1/4 tsp almond extract
>
>Optional: Candied cherries (page 25), powdered sugar, whole almonds, pine nuts, or chopped pistachios.

Preheat the oven to 350°, with convection, with a rack in the middle, or just above. Line two large cookie sheets with parchment paper.

Grind the almonds with the sugar in a food processor until very finely textured. Mix the eggs with the almond extract, and add to the almond mixture. Stir until uniform, ultimately using your hands.

Form 1-inch balls, and place at least an inch apart on the tray. Press a candied cherry or a whole almond into each ball, or roll in powered sugar, pine nuts, or chopped pistachios.

Bake for 13 – 14 minutes. Cool the tray on a wire rack for 20 minutes, then remove the cookies directly to the rack to finish cooling.

Notes:

>The cookies are *very* sensitive to the amount of egg white used – too much, and they will flatten out disappointingly. Measure!
>
>If you try to fit them all on one tray, they'll touch. Spend the extra 13 minutes to bake them in two batches.

Lemon Raspberry Cookies

These are the pinnacle of my efforts to create a more-or-less "standard" cookie, but without butter – I'm not a fan of buttery cookies. The lemon and raspberry take it to the next level, but if you left them out entirely you'd still have a perfectly decent cookie.

Yield: 2 crowded trays of cookies (about 48).

Dough:

  720 g flour (6 C)
  1 tsp baking powder
  1/4 tsp salt
  4 eggs
  1 1/3 C oil
  1 1/3 C sugar
  2 tsps vanilla
  3 tsps lemon oil
  zest from 2 lemons

Topping:

  10 oz raspberry jam
  1/2 C sugar

Mix the flour, baking powder, and salt in a large bowl.

In a separate bowl, mix together the eggs, oil, sugar, vanilla, and lemon oil, either with a whisk or an electric mixer, until smooth. Stir in the lemon zest, then add the wet ingredients to the dry, and mix, first with a wooden spoon, and then eventually with your hands, until the dough is uniform.

Form into balls about an inch in diameter (more or less), and flatten somewhat between your palms, placing each on an ungreased cookie sheet. They will expand a little, but not a lot, and can stand a little crowding – you should be able to get all the cookies arranged onto two trays.

Use your fingers to make a good-sized well in the center of each cookie (these will hold the jam, and the more jam the better…).

Preheat the oven to 350°, with convection, with a rack in the middle or just above.

Heat the jam and sugar in a small saucepan over a medium high heat until boiling, then lower the heat a little and boil for 4 – 5 minutes, stirring occasionally. Spoon the hot jam into the centers of the cookies, working quickly, as the jam will thicken as is cools.

Bake (in two batches) for about 14 minutes, and cool on wire racks.

Notes:

Lemon oil is strong stuff, and I've called for a lot of it. If you don't have lemons to zest you could try adding a little more – maybe 4 teaspoons instead of 3 – but if you overdo it the cookies will impart a not-so-pleasant tingling sensation.

If you don't have lemon oil, you could add the zest of another lemon or two – they will be fine, but not as lemony as with the oil.

The choice of jam undoubtedly matters; I use Polaner's seedless raspberry (which conveniently comes in 10 ounce jars).

You could certainly halve the recipe, if you were so inclined. (If instead you were to *increase* the recipe, you might have to stop and reheat the jam mixture to keep it flowing while you fill the cookies.)

Hermit Cookies

Spicy, chewy, delicious; a traditional New England favorite. Recipes vary quite a bit; mine has been carefully crafted to retain the consistency while eliminating the butter.

    2 C flour (240 g)
    1/4 tsp baking soda
    2 tsps cinnamon
    1 tsp ginger
    1/2 tsp cloves
    1/4 tsp nutmeg
    1/4 tsp allspice
    1 egg
    1/4 C oil
    3/4 C molasses
    1/2 C sugar
    1/2 tsp salt
    1 C raisins
    1/2 C chopped walnuts

Preheat the oven to 350°, with convection, with a rack in the upper middle.

Combine the flour, baking soda, and spices in a large mixing bowl. In another mixing bowl, use a fork to beat together the egg, oil, molasses, sugar, and salt until smooth. Add the wet mixture to the dry, along with the raisins and walnuts, and stir until uniform.

Line a large cookie sheet with parchment paper. Use a pair of tablespoons to dollop the batter into three logs, each running the length of the tray; even them out more or less, but don't work too hard – they are going to spread.

Bake for 17 or 18 minutes, then transfer (still on the parchment paper) to a rack to cool for about 15 minutes before peeling off the paper and slicing into cookies. Return the cookies to the rack to cool completely.

Tahini Sandwich Cookies

This recipe originates with the (now sadly defunct) *Common Ground* restaurant in Brattleboro, Vermont. Healthy and filling; these will get you through your day.

Yield: About 2 dozen sandwich cookies.

Cookies:

    3/4 C tahini (187 g)
    2/3 C honey (230 g)
    1/3 C barley malt syrup (115 g)
    1/2 tsp salt
    1 C sunflower seeds
    3 C rolled oats

Filling:

    1 C tahini (250 g)
    1/3 C honey (115 g)
    1/2 C peanut butter
    1/2 C carob powder

Preheat the oven to 350°, with convection, with a rack in the middle or just above. Line three large cookie sheets or half sheet pans with parchment paper.

Mix together the first four cookie ingredients, then mix in the sunflower seeds and rolled oats. The batter will be quite stiff. Drop by rounded teaspoonfuls onto one of the prepared pans. Flatten each cookie somewhat with slightly dampened hands. Bake for 12–14 minutes, until the cookies are golden brown all over, and the edges are just a little bit darkened. Let cool for 10 or 15 minutes before removing to racks. Repeat with the remaining cookies.

Mix the filling ingredients and divide between pairs of cookies after the cookies are thoroughly cooled. There is enough filling to be reasonably generous…

Note: Watch the cookies carefully during the last minute or two of baking – things happen fast… If you overcook them, they will be hard and crunchy (and still quite good), and if you undercook them, they will be a bit lacking in structure and that certain caramelized something that happens when foods darken (and also still quite good).

Ginsberg's Mandel Bread
*(with contributions by Marty, Butchie, and Hy Ginsberg;
optional raisins suggested by Gil Zucker.)*

Softer than its Italian cousin, mandel bread is essentially Jewish biscotti. The addition of raisins is decidedly untraditional ("Unheard of!" declared my grandfather, to which Gil Zucker replied "You just heard of it – *I* told you"). Make it how you like; I have come to prefer it with raisins.

> 4 eggs
> 1 1/2 C sugar
> 3/4 C oil
> 1 Tbs almond extract
> 1 Tbs Amaretto liqueur
> 1 tsp vanilla extract
> 2 1/4 tsp baking powder
> 1 tsp salt
> about 5 C flour (separated)
> 2 C coarsely chopped almonds
>
> Optional: 1 C raisins (mixed black and golden)

Preheat the oven to 330°, with convection, with a rack in the upper half. Lightly oil a large cookie sheet, or else line it with parchment paper.

In a large mixing bowl, cream the eggs and sugar; add the oil, almond extract, Amaretto, and vanilla, and mix well. Mix the baking powder and salt into 2 cups of the flour, and combine this with the egg mixture. Mix in the chopped almonds, and the raisins if using.

The amount of flour you ultimately require depends to a large extent on the size of your eggs. Start by adding 2 more cups. The batter should be quite sticky, but workable – you should be able to knead it briefly on a floured surface. If that is not yet the case, add more flour. Divide the batter in half, form each half into a long log, and place the logs lengthwise on the cookie sheet. (If you can't form logs that hold their shapes reasonably well, add more flour. You need not be able to knead the batter repeatedly like a dough – it should remain too sticky for that – but you should be able to work it into a reasonable log shape on a lightly floured surface.)

Bake for 35 – 40 minutes. Gently remove the loaves from the cookie sheet (and from the parchment paper), and cool on a rack for about 30 minutes.

Heat the oven to 350°, with convection. Use your sharpest serrated knife to cut the loaves into 3/4" slices, then bake the slices for 7 minutes on each side. (They will not all fit on one cookie sheet; you will have to bake them in two batches.) Cool on racks.

Note: Chopping the almonds coarsely is a challenge and a chore; the best method I have found so far is to arrange them one layer deep between two (uncoated) paper plates and gently smash them with a hammer, peaking under the top plate now and then to aim the next strike at anything still whole.

Lemon Bars
Adapted from the "The Tassajara Bread Book" by Edward Espe Brown.

These are an essential road trip food – nutritious, delicious, filling, and they keep well for weeks.

    1 1/2 C honey
    3 Tbs butter
    520 g whole wheat flour (4 1/3 C)
    1 Tbs baking powder
    finely grated zest from 3 lemons
    2 1/2 tsps cinnamon
    1/2 tsp cardamon
    1/4 tsp cloves
    1 1/2 C whole almonds (unblanched)

    Optional: 1/2 C candied lemon peel

Butter an 8 × 12 × 2 inch pan. Preheat the oven to 350°, without convection, with a rack in the middle, or just above.

Heat the honey and butter in a 3 quart saucepan over low heat until thin and liquidy. Combine all the remaining ingredients in a large mixing bowl, stir, and when the honey is ready, add the dry ingredients to the saucepan. Stir with your sturdiest wooden spoon until the batter is uniform (which takes a little elbow grease…), then transfer to the baking pan. Spread the batter evenly in the pan with your hands, washing your hands frequently to keep the batter from sticking to them (leaving them slightly damp after washing helps a little). Bake for 20 – 25 minutes (if they are dark around the edges after 20 minutes, call them done).

Cool in the pan on a wire rack for 5 minutes, then invert the pan over a cutting board to remove the bars. Slice into 24 bars (6 × 4), and cool these on a rack.

Note: You can use oranges instead of lemons; also good.

Rugelach

My great grandmother Becky's rugelach were amazing – wonderful – *legendary*. Sadly, *shockingly*, it seems that nobody ever recorded how she made them.

My cousin Marty, to his great credit, has devoted a great deal of effort and research into the discovery of a rugelach recipe that might be comparable to Becky's (and has concocted many fine batches of rugelach along the way); this recipe combines some of what I consider to be his best attempts, along with some minor adaptations of my own. In any case, ultimately we have Marty to thank for the recipe below, so thank you, Marty.

I was just a kid when I last had Becky's, and so I am not the best judge as to how authentic these are, but those more qualified than I are unfortunately a much-reduced and dwindling population. Such is life. In my best estimation, this is a reasonable re-creation of Becky's fine confection. They are, at the very least, delicious.

Yield: 48 small or 36 mid-sized rugelach.

Dough:

>   1 C lukewarm milk
>   2 1/4 tsps yeast
>   3 eggs (warmed in hot tap water)
>   1/4 C sugar
>   1/2 tsp salt
>   1/4 C softened butter
>   600 g flour (about 4 1/4 C)

Filling:

>   1 C sugar
>   1 C raisins
>   1 Tbs cinnamon
>   1 1/2 C walnuts
>
>   1/4 C melted butter, for brushing

Dissolve the yeast in the warm milk, then mix in the eggs, sugar, salt, and butter. Mix in flour until the dough becomes kneadable, then knead in the rest – the dough should be smooth, but not stiff. Cover and let rise (an hour and a half or two hours or so).

While the dough is rising, grind the sugar, raisins, and cinnamon together in a food processor, then add the walnuts and pulse until they are finely chopped. You should end up with about 3 cups of filling.

When the dough is ready, preheat the oven to 375°, without convection, with a shelf in the middle or just above, and lightly grease two half sheet pans or large cookie sheets. Divide the dough into 4 balls to make 48 small rugelach; 3 balls to make 36 larger rugelach.

For each ball of dough: Roll out (on a lightly floured surface) into a thin circle (about 1/8 inch thick) and brush with a little melted butter. If making 48 rugelach, spread with 3/4 of a cup of filling; if making 36 rugelach, spread with 1 cup of filling. Cut (like a pizza) into 12 triangles, and roll each one from the base to the point, curving slightly. Place on the prepared trays and bake for 10 – 13 minutes, until they begin to brown lightly on top. Cool on wire racks.

Note: *Rugelach* is plural; drop the "ch" at the end for the singular – one *rugelah*, two *rugelach*.

Angel Food Cake

The healthiest cake around – high protein, no fat. What a bonus that it also happens to be exceptionally delicious.

    415 g egg whites (1 3/4 C, from about 10 – 12 eggs)
    1 1/4 tsps cream of tartar
    1 1/3 C sugar (267 g)
    1/4 tsp salt
    1 1/4 tsps vanilla
    1/4 tsp almond extract
    1 C flour

After measuring the egg whites, preheat the oven to 375°, without convection, with a rack just below the middle.

In a very large mixing bowl, beat the egg whites with the cream of tartar to stiff peaks. Gradually beat in the sugar, then the salt, then the vanilla and almond extracts. Gently fold in the flour, a handful at a time, until all the flour is incorporated and the mixture is uniform.

Transfer the batter to an angel food cake pan, smooth the top, and rap sharply against the work surface a few times to collapse any air pockets. Bake for 35 minutes (don't open the oven early). Cool upside down.

You'll need a "knife" of some sort to remove the cake from the pan. As mine has a "nonstick" coating (a complete fallacy – it's hard to imagine the cake sticking more thoroughly to any other surface), I generally cut something suitable out of a paper plate. Free the sides first, then lift the cake up by the removable bottom of the pan, and slide your knife between the cake and the bottom, and between the cake and the central cone to complete the operation.

Notes:

    Conventional wisdom says that any speck of yolk in the eggs will adversely affect the results. I don't know if this is an exaggeration or not, but you may as well crack your eggs one at a time into a separate bowl, so that if you accidentally break a yolk, you can discard that one egg (without losing whatever you've accumulated so far).

    Have some patience when beating the egg whites; "stiff peaks" means that when you remove the beaters from the eggs, the resultant peaks remain pointing up straight – they don't tip over at all. This is all that provides structure to your cake, so don't skimp.

    There are plenty of good ways to serve an angel food cake, but for my money the best is topped with sliced strawberries. Stir a tablespoon or two of sugar into the strawberries a little while before serving to encourage them to release some liquid and create their own sauce. Whipped cream enthusiasts are invited to indulge.

Hy's Amazing Chocolate Bread

I can't even begin to tell you how good this is; you just have to make it and see.

Bread:

>473 g warm water (2 C)
>2 Tbs sugar
>1 1/2 tsps yeast
>2 tsps salt
>2 eggs
>850 g flour (about 7 C plus 4 tsps)

Filling:

>1 C sugar
>1/3 C cocoa powder
>4 Tbs butter

Topping:

>1 beaten egg
>1 - 2 Tbs turbinado sugar

Warm the eggs in a bowl of hot tap water. Add the sugar to the water in the bowl of a stand mixer (or a large mixing bowl), sprinkle in the yeast, and stir. Add a cup or two of flour, mix, then add the salt and eggs (beaten lightly), and mix again. Mix and/or knead in the rest of the flour: If you are using a stand mixer, add about half of the remaining flour, mix with the paddle attachment, then switch to the dough hook and add all but a tablespoon or two of the flour, process well, and finish kneading by hand (using the reserved bit of flour). Otherwise, gradually mix and then knead in the remaining flour by hand. Cover the bowl with plastic wrap and let rise for 1 - 2 hours.

Mix the sugar and cocoa for the filling, and melt the butter. Roll the dough out into a long rectangular or oblong shape, about 1/4 inch thick. Use the back of a tablespoon to spread the melted butter over the dough, leaving 1/2 inch unbuttered along one of the long edges. Sprinkle the sugar / cocoa mixture evenly over the dough, then roll the dough tightly toward the unbuttered edge, and pinch closed. Pinch the ends closed as well.

Butter a large cookie sheet or half sheet pan, then form the dough into a figure eight with the two ends tucked under the middle of the eight. Try to get the seams to face down on the sheet if possible. Brush with beaten egg and sprinkle with turbinado sugar. Cut shallow slits every inch or two, and let rise 20 or 30 minutes while the oven preheats. Bake at 375° (without convection) for about 30 minutes, in the middle of the oven, or just below.

Cinnamon Buns

Make the *Chocolate Bread* dough (page 42), and roll it out as in that recipe. Then:

Filling:

>2/3 C sugar
>4 tsps cinnamon
>4 Tbs butter

Preheat the oven to 375°, without convection, with a rack in the middle or just above. Butter two large cookie sheets.

Melt the butter and spread it over the dough, leaving about half an inch along one long edge. Mix together the sugar and cinnamon, and spread it evenly over the buttered dough. Roll the dough tightly toward the unbuttered edge, and pinch it closed. Cut into 3/4-inch wide buns with a sharp knife, and arrange these about 1/2 inch apart on the cookie sheets (they won't all fit on one). If you are inspired to brush these with some more melted butter, it can't hurt, but it's also not necessary. Bake in two batches, for about 20 minutes each, until lightly browned. Remove immediately to cooling racks, and serve warm.

Icing:

>3 C powdered sugar
>about 4 Tbs water

Add 3 tablespoons of water to the powdered sugar, stir, and then add more water, a little at a time, until a thick but smooth and spreadable icing forms. Serve with the buns – let your guests ice their own.

Notes:

>You could probably get away with less icing – maybe starting with 2 cups of powdered sugar – but it's annoying to run out and have to mix up more. So instead I have opted to overestimate.
>
>If these are not all consumed immediately and the icing develops a crust, just give it a stir and it will be as good as new.

The Best Chocolate Cake

Adapted from *Betty Crocker's Cookbook,* this excellent cake happens to be vegan – no eggs, no milk, no butter.

    1 2/3 C flour
    1 C sugar
    1/4 C cocoa powder
    1 tsp baking soda
    1/2 tsp salt
    1 C water
    1/3 C oil
    1 tsp vinegar
    1/2 tsp vanilla
    1/2 C semisweet chocolate chips

Preheat the oven to 350°, with convection, with a rack in the upper middle. Line the bottom of a 9 inch round cake pan with parchment paper.

Mix the dry ingredients and the wet ingredients separately, then pour the wet ingredients into the dry, along with the chocolate chips. Mix just until uniform, transfer to the cake pan, and jiggle a little to even out the batter. Bake for 35 – 40 minutes, until a toothpick inserted in the center comes out clean.

Allow the cake to cool completely in the pan. Then remove (by prising free the sides and carefully turning upside down – don't neglect to catch it…) and dust liberally with powdered sugar.

Notes:

    A stencil placed on the cake before dusting with powered sugar is an easy way to decorate (a nice trick for birthdays – it's easy to cut out a big "5"…).

    To double the recipe, make two cakes – trying to fill a larger pan leads to trouble cooking the cake properly.

    This recipe can be used to make a dozen (excellent) muffins; bake at 375° with convection for 16 – 18 minutes.

    Don't neglect the vinegar – it's needed to activate the baking soda.

Valeria's Italian Orange Cake

Valeria's family recipe, from Roma.

>   3 eggs
>   2/3 C sugar
>   zest of 2 oranges
>   3/4 C fresh orange juice (from about 2 oranges)
>   1 Tbs orange liqueur (such as *Grand Marnier*)
>   1/3 C oil
>   1/2 tsp salt
>   1 2/3 C flour
>   1 Tbs baking powder
>   powdered sugar

Separate the eggs (do this first, before preparing the oranges, so that the whites have a chance to warm to room temperature – they will beat a little better).

Prepare the oranges, then preheat the oven to 350°, without convection, with a rack in the middle or just above. Grease and flour a 9 inch round cake pan.

Beat the egg yolks and sugar in a medium sized mixing bowl until fairly smooth and significantly lightened in color. Mix in the orange zest, juice, liqueur, oil, and salt. Add the flour and baking powder, and mix slowly, just until combined.

Clean and dry the beaters well, and beat the egg whites to stiff peaks. Gently fold the beaten egg whites into the rest of the batter until uniform, and pour into the prepared cake pan. Bake for about 30 minutes, until a toothpick inserted in the center comes out clean. Cool for at least 10 minutes before removing from the pan.

When the cake is completely cool, dust with powdered sugar.

Notes:

>   Valeria makes this gluten-free using rice flour; she also uses a little more salt (3/4 tsp).
>
>   Not all oranges are created equal – buy an extra, in case yours are not particularly juicy.

Ice Cream Sandwiches

Homemade ice cream sandwiches – a revelation!

    6 Tbs butter, melted
    1/2 C sugar
    1/3 C cocoa powder
    1/2 C plus 2 Tbs flour
    3/4 tsp baking soda
    1/4 tsp salt
    1 egg
    1 tsp vanilla
    1 Tbs water
    vanilla ice cream (1/2 gallon is plenty)

Preheat the oven to 350° (with or without convection), with a rack in the middle, or just above. Line a large cookie sheet with parchment paper.

Combine the sugar, cocoa powder, flour, baking soda, and salt in a medium mixing bowl. Lightly beat the egg with the water and vanilla in a small bowl. Stir the melted butter into the dry ingredients, then add the egg mixture, and mix until uniform. Use a rubber spatula to spread the batter evenly on the cookie sheet, not quite going all the way to the edges.

Bake for 10 minutes. Allow to cool completely before slicing into 16 or 24 rectangles (for 8 or 12 sandwiches, respectively). Transfer these to a plastic bag, with parchment or wax paper between the layers to prevent sticking, and freeze for at least an hour before filling with ice cream.

There are two schools of thought regarding filling the sandwiches. One way is to turn the ice cream out onto a plastic cutting board, slice it into rectangular slabs, and fit these into the sandwiches. The other is to scoop the ice cream into the sandwiches, and massage it into shape with a spoon or knife. Both are trickier than they sound, and quite impressively messy. I've come to favor the slicing method; if you decide to go that route, you can improve your experience a bit by freezing the cutting board beforehand.

Whichever way you choose to make a mess, wrap each sandwich individually in plastic wrap, and return to the freezer.

Note: The recipe assumes you will use "natural" cocoa powder (in which category both *Hershey's* and *Ghirardelli* fall); if you use "Dutch process" (or "processed with alkali") cocoa powder, replace the baking soda with baking *powder*.

Date Balls
Adapted from "The Tassajara Bread Book" by Edward Espe Brown.

These grow on you, and may become addictive. Don't say I didn't warn you…

- 2 C pitted dates (10 oz)
- 1 C raisins (5.5 oz)
- 1/2 C plus 1 Tbs carob powder
- 1/4 C sesame seeds, toasted and ground

Put the dates, raisins, and carob powder into a food processor, and blend until it comes together into a solid, fairly uniform mass – it takes a little while. Then form into small balls, about 3/4 inch in diameter, rolling each one in the sesame seeds.

Notes:

It is not so uncommon for a batch of "pitted" dates to contain one or two dates with pits. Check each one carefully; a chopped up pit makes these a lot less appealing.

Use an extra tablespoon or two of carob powder if the dates are especially moist.

Although the food processor will appear to be a disastrous, uncleanable mess after making these, if you let it soak in warm water for a little while, it's really not so bad.

Nut Balls
Adapted from "The New Book of Middle Eastern Food" by Claudia Roden.

300 g almonds
1 C sugar
2 – 3 Tbs rose water or orange blossom water
powdered sugar

Finely grind the almonds with the sugar in a food processor. Add 2 tablespoons of the rose or orange blossom water and process just to mix. Transfer to a bowl and mix with your hands, adding more rose or orange blossom water as needed until the mixture holds together well. Form into balls, about 3/4 inch in diameter, and roll these in powdered sugar to coat.

Vanilla or Chocolate Pudding
Adapted from "Betty Crocker's Cookbook."

Pudding takes a little patience (but is well worth it!). And there's some artistry required: On the one hand, you want to be very careful not to burn the bottom – so you have to cook it over a low heat. On the other, you want it to boil during your lifetime, so you have to cook it over a high heat... In the end, you have to figure out the right balance. Start with something you'd call "medium," or maybe slightly hotter. Definitely use a heavy bottomed saucepan, and stir pretty much constantly (at first, when the milk is still cold, you can get away with less – so you can separate the eggs, for example, while the pudding starts to heat).

Yield: 6 very generous or 8 more modest servings.

For vanilla pudding:

    2/3 C sugar
    1/4 C corn starch
    2 tsp vanilla

For chocolate pudding:

    1 C sugar
    3 Tbs corn starch
    2/3 C cocoa powder
    1 tsp vanilla

For both:

    4 C milk
    3 egg yolks, lightly beaten
    1/4 tsp salt

Mix the sugar, corn starch, salt, and (for chocolate) cocoa in a heavy bottomed saucepan. Whisk in a little of the milk, then the rest. Cook, stirring constantly, until it begins to boil, then continue to cook, stirring, for one minute.

Remove the pan from the heat. The next step is to "temper" the yolks; continue to stir frequently while you do this – the pudding can still burn, even while it's off the heat. Add a small amount of the hot pudding to the yolks – a smaller volume than that of the yolks themselves – stirring as you do so. Then stir a somewhat larger volume of pudding into the yolk mixture, and repeat until you've added a few good ladle-fuls of pudding. Then stir the yolk mixture back into the pudding. Return to the heat, and cook, stirring, until the pudding returns to a boil. Boil, stirring, for one minute, then remove from the heat, stir in the vanilla, and pour into ramekins or small bowls. Chill before serving.

Indian Pudding
Adapted from Stacy Brooks' "Tangled Up in Food" blog.

Jerry Garcia once said that the Grateful Dead are "like licorice – not everybody likes licorice, but the people who like licorice *really* like licorice." Well, Indian pudding is like the Grateful Dead, who are like licorice. I love all three…

    3 C milk
    1/3 C cornmeal
    1/4 C molasses
    1/4 C sugar
    1/2 tsp salt
    1/4 tsp cinnamon
    1/2 tsp ginger

    vanilla ice cream

Preheat the oven to 275°, without convection, with a rack in the middle or just above. Grease a 2 quart casserole dish.

Scald the milk over medium heat. Gradually stir in the cornmeal and molasses, and continue to cook, stirring, until thickened and just beginning to boil, about 10 minutes (more or less, depending on how hot your burner is and when you decided the milk was scalding). Remove from the heat and stir in the remaining ingredients.

Transfer to the prepared casserole dish, and bake until a thin skin forms, about 1 hour and 45 minutes. Serve warm, topped with vanilla ice cream.

Rice Pudding
Adapted from "Betty Crocker's Cookbook."

There are two things you can do with leftover rice; this is one of them (the other is on page 237). Of course you can make fresh rice to make rice pudding, but that would leave just one thing to do with leftover rice…

    2 C cooked rice
    2 eggs
    1/2 C sugar
    1/2 C raisins
    2 C milk
    1/2 tsp vanilla
    1/4 tsp salt
    ground nutmeg

Preheat the oven to 325°, without convection, with a rack in the middle or just above.

You can mix everything together in the (ungreased) 1 1/2 quart casserole dish in which you will bake the pudding, or you can do it in a mixing bowl and transfer it. In any case, lightly beat the eggs, then mix in everything else except the nutmeg. Transfer to the casserole dish (if it isn't already there), and sprinkle with nutmeg.

In total you will bake the pudding for 50 minutes, but remove it from the oven and give it a good stirring twice – once after 20 minutes, and again after another 20 minutes. By the second stirring it will have some structure (that you will break up); ten minutes later it's done. Don't overcook.

Let sit for at least 15 minutes to serve it warm; or else refrigerate and serve chilled – it is excellent both ways.

Tapioca Pudding
Adapted from the "Bob's Red Mill" tapioca package.

Tapioca is a starch made from the cassava root, and then sometimes pressed into "pearls." Either small or large pearl tapioca will suffice for this excellent pudding (but do not use the crushed "minute" tapioca that is commonly used to thicken pies). Pudding made from small pearl tapioca has a smoother texture; my family unanimously prefers large pearl – it's just more fun…

I like to make a vast quantity when I make tapioca pudding, as leftovers make an excellent snack cold from the fridge, but if you want to show some restraint, halve the recipe.

Yield: About 2 quarts.

> 2/3 C small or large pearl tapioca
> 1 1/2 C water
> 4 1/2 C milk
> 1/2 tsp salt
> 4 eggs, separated
> 1 C sugar
> 1 tsp vanilla

Place the tapioca and water in a large (at least 3 quarts), heavy bottomed saucepan, and leave to soak for half an hour.

Add the milk, salt, and lightly beaten egg yolks, and bring to a boil, stirring more or less constantly, over medium high heat. Reduce to a simmer, and continue to cook, stirring frequently, for 15 minutes.

While the pudding is simmering, beat the egg whites with the sugar to form soft peaks. It will probably take the full 15 minutes; the stiffer you can get them the better, and don't forget to stir the pudding while you beat the eggs… You can stir with one hand while continuing to beat the egg whites with the other; this is an impressive feat to witness, should any casual observers happen to pass by.

When the egg whites are ready, fold in a ladle-full of hot tapioca, and then repeat a few times, bringing the egg white mixture up to temperature a bit. Then fold the egg whites gently into the tapioca, and stir over medium low heat for about three minutes – the mixture should have returned to some semblance of a simmer.

Remove from the heat, cool for 15 minutes, and then stir in the vanilla. You can then pour the pudding into individual bowls or ramekins, if you have enough, or else just pour all of it into a suitably sized casserole dish. It is delicious served warm, and also excellent chilled. (Refrigerate, of course, once it has cooled sufficiently.)

Breakfast

Granola

There is no shortage of excellent granola recipes; here's mine. Crunchy, delicious, with just the right amount of sweetness.

>3 C rolled oats
>3/4 C slivered almonds
>3/4 C cashew pieces
>1/2 C pumpkin seeds
>1/2 C sunflower seeds
>1/3 C wheat germ
>2 tsps cinnamon
>3/4 C honey (260g)
>5/8 tsp salt
>3 Tbs vegetable oil

Preheat the oven to 300°, with convection. In a large mixing bowl, mix together the oats, nuts, pumpkin seeds, sunflower seeds, wheat germ, and cinnamon. Put the honey in a small, microwave-proof bowl, and microwave on high for about 40 seconds. Stir in the salt until dissolved, then the oil, and pour over the dry ingredients. Stir until everything is evenly coated.

Line a half sheet pan with parchment paper, and spread the granola evenly in the pan. Bake in the top middle of the oven for 40 – 45 minutes – without stirring – until nicely browned. (Better to err on the side of overcooking – if the granola isn't cooked long enough, it won't be as crunchy.) Cool completely before breaking into pieces.

Note: All of the nuts and seeds should be raw and unsalted.

Chocolate Granola

Chocolate granola – a reason to get up in the morning.

    4 C rolled oats (regular, not "quick" or "instant")
    2 C slivered almonds
    2/3 C sugar
    pinch salt
    1/2 C water
    50 ml oil (50 ml is 1/4 C minus 2 tsp)
    1 C semisweet chocolate chips (155 g)
    4 C puffed rice

Preheat the oven to 325°, with convection, with a shelf in the middle or just above.

Mix the oats and almonds together in a large mixing bowl.

Combine the sugar, salt, water, and oil in a small saucepan, and bring to a boil. Turn off the heat (but leave the pan on the burner) and add the chocolate chips, stirring until fully dissolved. If necessary, heat very gently. Pour the chocolate mixture over the oats and almonds and stir; add the puffed rice and mix until everything is well coated.

Divide the granola between two ungreased 8 × 12 × 2 inch baking trays, and bake until fully dried, about 40 minutes, stirring every 10 minutes. Cool before bagging.

Pancakes

Serve these with *real* maple syrup, please.

Serves 3.

>   2 1/2 C flour (300 g)
>   2 tsps baking powder
>   1 tsp salt
>   2 eggs
>   2 C milk (490 g)
>   1/4 C oil

Mix the dry and wet ingredients separately, then add the wet to the dry and stir to combine.

You can't make a proper pancake in a nonstick frying pan – the "skin" comes out all wrong. Heat a heavy frying pan (stainless steel or cast iron work well) until a drop of water sizzles instantly, then pour in a small amount of oil and immediately spread the oil around the pan with a paper towel, wiping out any excess. This very thin coat of oil is all you'll need to keep the pancakes from sticking (and you only need to do it this once, at the beginning – you can put the oil away now).

The key to pancake making is maintaining the perfect temperature in your pan. Too hot, and the outsides will darken or even burn before the insides cook. Too cool, and they won't "set" properly (and you'll be standing there for hours). You'll have to practice, and if you lose a batch in the process, it's a small price to pay. As you cook them, you will probably have to gradually turn the heat down a bit – the perfect setting when you start cooking will very likely eventually become too hot.

Spoon the batter into the pan; multiple, small pancakes cook a little easier than a single large one does, and offer your diners the opportunity to share a batch more easily, and to control portion size more precisely. But it's up to you. Flip the pancakes over when bubbles have appeared throughout, and when the edges have started to dry out some. Cook until the second side is done and the pancakes are cooked through. Serve immediately. (Sorry, but the cook eats last, when the cooking is all done…)

Notes:

>   If you have the time and the patience, let the batter sit for a little while – up to an hour – before frying. If not, fine.

Fruit pancakes are good, but present additional cooking challenges. In the end, I think that for strawberry or banana pancakes, you're better off making regular pancakes, then topping them with sliced strawberries or bananas (and maple syrup, of course). That doesn't work so well with blueberries, so I give some advice for blueberry pancakes below.

You can decrease the flour to 2 cups (240 g) for a thinner, more crepe-like pancake – these are also very good (and preferred by some…), and they cook a little faster and more easily.

Variations:

Buttermilk Pancakes: Use 1 C buttermilk and 1 C milk.

Blueberry Pancakes: Add 2 C fresh blueberries. Make sure the blueberries are reasonably dry and at room temperature – or warmer – before adding them to the batter (cold, wet spots in the batter are harder to cook thoroughly). You might need a little additional oil every now and then, as blueberries burst while cooking and leave a residue that burns to the pan.

Gingerbread Pancakes: Inspired by the *Penny Cluse Cafe* in Burlington, Vermont (go there if you can!); these are amazing. To the dry ingredients, add:

- 2 tsps cinnamon
- 1/2 tsp ginger
- 1/4 tsp nutmeg
- 1/4 tsp cloves
- 1 Tbs sugar

Pecan Pancakes: Add 2 C chopped pecans.

Chocolate Chip Pancakes: For the record, I am morally opposed. But they are always popular with the kids. If you must make them, I suggest using semi-sweet chocolate chips. If you can get away with it, make regular pancakes, and just sprinkle chocolate chips on some of them when you first put the batter in the pan. Otherwise, add them straight to the batter – about 1 C should do.

Waffles
Adapted from "Betty Crocker's Cookbook."

2 C flour (240 g)
4 tsps baking powder
1/2 tsp salt
2 C milk
2 eggs
1/2 C oil

Mix the dry and wet ingredients separately, then add the wet to the dry and stir to combine. Cook in a preheated waffle iron.

Note: If you can let the batter sit a little while – up to an hour – before making the waffles, all the better (if not, it will still be fine).

Variations:

Buttermilk Waffles: Use 1 C buttermilk and 1 C milk.

Pecan Waffles: Add 1 – 2 C chopped pecans.

Multigrain Waffles: Use 1 1/4 C flour, 1/2 C whole wheat flour, and 1/4 C cornmeal.

Dutch Baby Pancake

Terrible name. But delicious nonetheless. And impressive to look at.

You need a 14 inch cast iron skillet to make this (measure across the *bottom*) – you really do, it won't come out right in a smaller one. You can halve the recipe and make it in a 10 inch cast iron skillet, but if you do that there's not a whole lot to go around – after all, there's not much more substance to this than the eggs, and three eggs don't serve too many people…

6 eggs
1 C flour
1 C milk
1/4 tsp salt
1/8 tsp nutmeg
2–3 Tbs butter
1 fresh lemon
powdered sugar

Preheat the oven to 425°, without convection, with a rack about a quarter of the way up from the bottom (as the pancake cooks it rises considerably, and the top edges can burn if it's too high). You can put the cast iron pan in the oven while it preheats; this will save you a little time when you're ready to bake.

Whisk together the eggs, flour, milk, salt, and nutmeg until they form a smooth batter. If your pan isn't hot yet, put it in the preheated oven for about 10 minutes.

Take the hot pan out of the oven, put the butter in it, and swirl it around until the butter is fully melted and evenly spread across the bottom and most of the way up the sides. Then pour in the batter, return the pan to the oven, and bake for 20 minutes.

When it's done, transfer it from the pan to a cutting board with a pair of metal spatulas. Dust it liberally with powdered sugar, and squeeze the lemon over it. Serve immediately.

Notes:

> If you don't have a lemon, an orange will do (especially if it's a bit sour). If all you have is prepared lemon (or orange) juice, I think you'd be better off just omitting it.

> Some people add a little sugar to the batter; I vote no…

Salads, Snacks, Sauces, Spreads, Etc.

Caesar Salad

A true classic. Here I have replaced the customary croutons with "toasted bread cubes"; these have a nice "tooth" to them, but don't shatter when pierced with a fork, and are not salted or spiced. They absorb a little of the dressing, but don't get soggy. And I have eschewed the traditional "coddled" egg for the safer alternative of mayonnaise, with no compromise in quality. Anchovy enthusiasts are invited to indulge, but it is still a great salad without them.

Salad:

    romaine lettuce, rinsed, drained, and cut or torn
    pecorino romano cheese, coarsely grated or thinly sliced

    Optional: sliced anchovies, to garnish

Dressing:

    1/2 C mayonnaise
    1 Tbs fresh lemon juice
    1 small garlic clove, crushed
    1/2 tsp dijon mustard
    1/2 tsp worcestershire sauce
    pinch or two salt
    a few grinds black pepper

    Optional: 1/2 tsp anchovy paste

Bread Cubes:

    white bread, preferably a little stale, cut into cubes
    olive oil

Preheat the broiler, with a rack in the middle of the oven. Drizzle the bread cubes with a little olive oil, stir, and repeat once or twice. The goal is to lightly coat the bread cubes with oil, without soaking them. They can be a little bare in some spots, and a little oily in others – it will even out somewhat in the oven. Spread them on a baking sheet and broil for a minute or two, watching carefully, until they start to brown. Remove the baking sheet from the oven, shake and stir the bread, trying to get the brown parts of the cubes facing any direction other than up, and return to the oven for another minute, again watching carefully, until they start to brown again. Repeat this process one more time if you have the patience, otherwise call it good enough. Set the toasted bread cubes aside.

Mix together all the dressing ingredients.

Mix the lettuce with a generous handful of cheese. Just before serving toss the salad with some of the dressing – how much depends on how much lettuce you are using. Mix in a tablespoon or two at a time, until the salad is well dressed, but not sopping. Add the bread cubes and toss some more, then sprinkle on some more romano cheese (and decorate with anchovies, if you are so inclined).

Notes:

Traditional worcestershire sauce contains a small amount of anchovies, so make sure to use a vegetarian version if you're morally opposed.

Sometimes it's nice to go a little heavy on the mustard. And if you're feeling lazy, a little garlic powder can take the place of the fresh clove. If, on the other hand, you are feeling ambitious, grinding the garlic and salt into a paste in a mortar and pestle makes it extra special; be sure to scrape every little bit out with your tiniest rubber spatula.

Sour Garlic Pickles

A family tradition, the making of sour garlic pickles includes a bit of alchemy the origin of which is long forgotten: the slice of bread that tops the brine. Does it really contribute anything to the results, or is it just superstition, whimsy, or some clever ancestor's technique for keeping out flies? The answer could of course be easily determined by experiment, but I am not inclined to investigate – my grandparents and great grandparents topped their pickle jars with bread, and that is good enough for me.

A word of warning to the uninitiated – these are not your gherkins or dills, and if you've never had a real sour garlic pickle before, then you may find them somewhat shocking. I don't guarantee that you'll like them, but if you do, then you will probably *really* like them…

They can be made with any kind of cucumber, but "kirbys" are traditional; choose especially firm specimens. As mentioned above, in addition to the cucumbers you will need a slice of bread (ideally rye, but french, white, or sourdough are all reasonable alternatives) for each jar.

Brine, per quart of water:

> 40 g kosher salt
> 3 – 5 large garlic cloves
> 2 – 3 tsps whole black peppercorns

Wash the cucumbers well, and pack them tightly into glass jars – the tighter the better. Estimate the amount of brine needed to fill the jars, and scale the recipe above accordingly. Mix the salt into the water until it is dissolved. Cut off the bases of the garlic cloves, bruise them slightly with the heel of a knife, and remove the skins. Pour the brine into the jars, completely covering the cucumbers, and leaving 1/4 – 1/2 inch of head space at the top. Distribute the garlic cloves and peppercorns more or less evenly between the jars. Cut a slice of bread to roughly fit the opening of each jar, and lay it on top, in the brine. Partially cover each jar, and let sit for somewhere between 3 and 7 days (depending on the weather, the variety of cucumber, and the mysteries of the universe), until the pickles have yellowed significantly and are distinctly sour smelling. Remove what you can of the bread, completely cover the jars, and refrigerate.

Photos: On the left: day one; on the right: day six.

Vietnamese Cucumber Salad
Adapted from "Pleasures of the Vietnamese Table" by Mai Pham.

Start this a few hours before dinner, as it benefits from marinating for a while.

    6 small, pickling cucumbers, peeled and sliced 1/8 inch thick
    2 shallots, thinly sliced
    6 sprigs cilantro, chopped
    1/4 C rice vinegar
    1 Tbs lime juice
    3 Tbs sugar
    1/2 tsp salt

Combine the vinegar, lime juice, sugar, and salt in a small bowl, and mix well. Pour over the vegetables, and stir to coat. Refrigerate until 15 or 20 minutes before serving, stirring once or twice if you happen to think of it.

Notes:

It may initially seem dry, but the sugar draws liquid from the cucumbers – it will ultimately be plenty juicy.

If you can't find pickling cucumbers you can make this with 2 larger cucumbers; cut them in half lengthwise and scoop out the seeds with a spoon before slicing them.

Candied Nuts

There are numerous ways to candy nuts; this method is easy, relatively quick, and delicious. Pecans, walnuts, and pistachios all work well, and the results make an excellent addition to a salad.

    1 1/3 C nuts (raw, unsalted)
    1/4 C sugar
    1 Tbs butter
    1/4 tsp salt

Put everything together in a small, nonstick frying pan and stir over medium heat until the sugar is liquid and the nuts are well coated. Transfer to a sheet of parchment paper and immediately separate the nuts (they solidify quickly). They're ready once they're cool.

Marmalade

This is the best marmalade you ever had, bar none. It's not overly sweet (thanks to the generous use of lemons and some restraint with the sugar), and it is *full* of delicious chunks of peel.

Sizes of oranges and lemons vary, so the quantities are approximate, but the idea is to end up with about twice as much orange as lemon (by volume). Choosing oranges with very few seeds lessens the work considerably; valencia or cara cara oranges work well. And I have used both regular and meyer lemons with good results. If you can find organic oranges and lemons, all the better, since you will be using all of the peel (along with the rest of the fruit).

Aside from cutting the fruit, it's basically the same amount of work to make a lot as it is to make a little, so this recipe makes a lot. Give some away, you'll be very popular.

Yield: About 10 – 11 cups.

    8 medium large oranges
    6 small lemons
    water and sugar, as directed below

Wash and thinly slice the oranges and lemons (about 1/16 – 1/8 of an inch thick), using the whole fruits, discarding only the seeds, any blemishes, and the two end bits. Cut the fruit slices into sections as you go (quarters for the lemons and eighths for the oranges is about right). Save any pulp that falls off the peel, as well as all of the juice. You should end up with approximately twice as much orange as lemon, with about 8 cups of orange (peel, pulp, and juice combined), and 4 cups of lemon.

Put all of the fruit into a large, deep pot, and cover with a little less water than there is fruit – for 12 cups of fruit, use about 10 cups of water; 11 if the fruit wasn't juicy. Bring to a boil, then simmer for 5 minutes, stirring occasionally. Cover, and refrigerate overnight.

Place a small plate in the freezer. You will know that the marmalade is done when a small amount spread on the cold plate gels into the consistency you'd expect in the finished product. It might take a little practice to judge, so if you're uncertain, let the approximate boiling time (30 minutes) influence your assessment.

Prepare your jars – wash and carefully dry them, and have a few more than you think you'll need.

Return the pot to the stove, bring to a boil, and boil (uncovered) over high heat, stirring occasionally, until the peels are soft, about 45 minutes. Then measure how much you have, and add a little less sugar than you have fruit mixture – 1 to 1 1/2 cups less, assuming you started with about 12 cups of fruit. (You should be down to somewhere in the vicinity of 11 cups of fruit, so you are adding about 10 cups of sugar, more or less.) Return to a rapid boil, and continue to boil – stirring frequently, especially as it thickens – until it's properly gelled, about 30 minutes or so.

The marmalade is now done; if you're going to can it, then you have a fair amount of work ahead of you… (There are excellent instructions in the *Ball Blue Book – Guide to Home Canning, Freezing, and Dehydration*.) I rarely bother, instead I ladle the marmalade into the jars and store them in the refrigerator.

Notes:

The ladling is unavoidably messy; clean up the rims with moist paper towels before capping the jars. And leave about 1/4 to 1/2 inch of headroom – it helps the jars seal better.

If you let the final boiling continue for too long, you'll end up with a solid mass of unspreadable marmalade…Still delicious, but a bit of a disappointment. The voice of experience: 45 minutes is *way* too long, and when I go to 35 minutes, I usually wish I had stopped 5 minutes sooner…

Modica

Modica ("moo-DEE-cah") is a (delicious) mix of ground, toasted almonds and breadcrumbs, suitable for sprinkling on pasta, vegetables, seafood, or whatever else you like. (Pasta with olive oil, modica, and grated cheese is a simple treat.) I learned how to make it from my friend Jackie, who learned from her grandmother, who presumably brought the "recipe" over from Italy. I can find no reference to it on the internet, so perhaps we are preserving a bit of cultural history here.

>   3 parts almonds
>   1 part breadcrumbs
>   olive oil
>
>   Optional: a bit of cinnamon

Roast the almonds in a 375° oven, stirring occasionally, until they are well browned throughout (break one in half now and then to check).

Toast the breadcrumbs in a pan with a small amount of olive oil until they are as dark as the almonds.

Grind the almonds in a food processor, then add the breadcrumbs (and cinnamon, if using), and process just to mix.

Notes:

>   I use seasoned breadcrumbs, which I suspect is not authentic, but the results are excellent nonetheless. And I omit the cinnamon.
>
>   Modica keeps indefinitely in the refrigerator.

Peanut Sauce
Adapted from "Vegetarian Cooking for Everyone" by Deborah Madison.

Excellent on tofu, rice, and vegetables.

Yield: About 7/8 of a cup.

> 6 Tbs (1/4 C plus 2 Tbs) natural peanut butter (just peanuts and perhaps salt)
> 2 Tbs rice vinegar
> 2 tsps brown sugar (packed)
> 4 tsps soy sauce
> 1/2 tsp salt
> 1/4 tsp garlic powder
> 1/4 – 1/2 C water
>
> Optional: 1/2 – 1 tsp chile oil (a.k.a. hot sesame oil)

Mix together all of the ingredients except the water, until well blended and smooth. Add 1/4 cup of water, mix well, and then thin with additional water as desired.

Notes:

> I use peanut butter that has a little salt; if yours doesn't, you might want to increase the salt slightly.

> I actually use more like 1/2 teaspoon of coarsely ground garlic – more like sand than powder – and I don't really measure… If you have that around, great, but if not, just use what you have – 1/4 teaspoon of powder is probably about right.

Tahini Yogurt Sauce
Adapted from "Vegetarian Cooking for Everyone" by Deborah Madison.

The perfect topping for mujadara (see page 233).

    1 C yogurt
    3 Tbs tahini
    a small garlic clove, crushed
    1/4 tsp salt
    1 Tbs fresh lemon juice

If you have the patience, grind the garlic and salt together with a mortar and pestle, then mix everything together. If you don't, then just mix everything together… (If you want to leave the garlic out entirely, that will also be okay.)

Note: Use "regular" yogurt – not Greek.

Cucumber Yogurt Sauce

This is essentially Greek "tzatziki" sauce, except that I prefer regular yogurt to Greek, and tzatziki sauce usually includes herbs such as dill or mint, which I omit. (See photo, page 194.)

    2 C yogurt
    1 medium cucumber
    2 Tbs olive oil
    1 clove garlic, crushed
    pinch or two of salt

Peel the cucumber, slice it lengthwise, and use a spoon to scrape out the middle part with the seeds. Grate the remainder on a box grater, then mix all of the ingredients together. Keep refrigerated until ready to serve.

Note: Try to make the sauce at least a few hours before you serve it, so the flavors have time to meld.

Surfer Spread

This is my take on the stuff of the same name that they make at the *Brattleboro Food Coop* in Brattleboro, Vermont. Healthy and delicious.

Yield: About 2 cups.

>	1 (14 oz) block of firm or extra firm tofu
>	3/4 C sun-dried tomatoes, packed in oil
>	1 tsp garlic powder
>	2 tsps dijon mustard
>	4 tsps nutritional yeast
>	4 tsps tamari (or soy sauce)
>	greens from 4 scallions, chopped

Process all of the ingredients except the scallions in a food processor, scraping the sides as necessary, until the mixture is relatively smooth – some small chunks of sun-dried tomatoes should remain. Add the scallions and process just a little more, until the scallions are finely ground. Refrigerate.

Mint Julep

As Anne describes it, "a good mood in a glass."

How much mint is in a "bunch" is anyone's guess… It doesn't much matter – your mint syrup will be stronger if it's a lot, subtler if it's not. (Of course if you have a *whole lot*, decide that it's 2 or 3 bunches, and scale up the recipe accordingly.)

Mint Syrup:

>	1 bunch fresh mint – leaves only (no stems)
>	1 C water
>	1 C sugar

Mix the sugar and water in a saucepan, bring to a boil, and boil without stirring for 5 minutes. Pour the hot syrup over the mint leaves, and crush them somewhat with the back of a metal spoon. Transfer to a glass jar and refrigerate overnight. Then strain out and discard the mint leaves and return the syrup to the refrigerator.

Note: I have yet to transfer the syrup from the pot to the jar without making a sticky mess. Try to do better. Good luck.

Per Drink:

>	2 shots bourbon
>	2 shots mint syrup
>	crushed ice
>	
>	Optional: 1 or 2 fresh mint leaves plus a sprig to garnish

If you have fresh mint leaves, place 1 or 2 in the bottom of a medium sized glass (about 10 oz. or so), and bruise them gently with the back of a spoon. Fill the glass with crushed ice, then add the bourbon and the mint syrup, and stir. Top it up with more crushed ice, and serve with a straw and a mint sprig.

Notes:

>	This is why we grow mint… (It is infamous for spreading, so if you plant some, make sure it's in an area that is naturally contained, or you are likely to have it everywhere.)

If it's summer, try to make sure to have some fresh mint for the garnish – it's definitely more impressive. But if not, pour a glass anyway and enjoy.

It doesn't really matter how big a "shot" is – you want roughly equal amounts of bourbon and mint syrup, and you can choose your glass size so that it all fits…

Quickbread

Drop Biscuits

When you need some bread for dinner but didn't think about it in advance, these are the ticket – you can prepare them while the oven preheats, and they're ready 15 minutes after they go in.

Yield: About 12 biscuits.

> 420 g flour (3 1/2 C)
> 3 tsps baking powder
> 1 1/2 tsps salt
> 1 1/2 C milk
> 3 Tbs oil

Preheat the oven to 450°, without convection, with a rack in the middle or just above. Line a large cookie sheet with parchment paper (or lightly grease it).

Mix together the dry ingredients. Mix the oil and milk (disregarding the obvious impossibility of this feat), add the wet ingredients to the dry, and mix just until uniform. Drop by hugely heaping tablespoons onto the cookie sheet, and bake for 12 – 15 minutes, until browned in spots. Serve warm.

Strawberry Muffins

Truly excellent…

Yield: 12 muffins.

    2 1/2 C flour (300 g)
    1/2 C sugar
    3 tsps baking powder
    1 tsp salt
    3/4 C buttermilk
    1/2 C milk
    1/2 C oil
    1 egg
    1 1/2 C thinly sliced strawberries

Preheat the oven to 400°, with convection, with a rack in the upper middle. Line a muffin tin with paper muffin cups.

Mix the dry ingredients and the wet ingredients separately, then mix them together, along with the strawberries. Divide evenly among the muffin cups, and bake for 18-20 minutes.

Melissa's Blueberry Muffins

These are not your average blueberry muffins. They are more work, and use more blueberries, but they're the best, and well worth it.

I don't know where Melissa found this recipe (so I can't give credit back any farther than her); in any case I have made a number of changes (so technically these are "Melissa and Hy's," but it's my name on the book, so you probably figured that out already…).

Be sure to start the butter softening long before you're ready to get to work.

    3 C fresh blueberries, divided
    2 1/2 C flour (300 g)
    2 1/2 tsps baking powder
    1 tsp salt
    4 Tbs butter, softened
    1 C plus 2 Tbs sugar, divided
    1/4 C oil
    2 eggs
    1 C buttermilk
    1 1/2 tsps vanilla
    grated zest of 2 lemons
    2 Tbs turbinado sugar

Grease the top of a muffin tin, and line it with paper muffin cups.

Mix together the flour, baking powder, and salt.

Use an electric mixer to cream the butter with 1 cup of the sugar (as best you can – it's not entirely possible…), then beat in the oil, eggs, buttermilk, and vanilla.

Preheat the oven to to 425°, with convection, with a rack just above the middle.

Add the wet ingredients to the dry, mix briefly, and add 2 cups of the blueberries. Mix, and then divide the batter among the muffin cups – it will pretty much fill them. Level and slightly depress the tops of the muffins in preparation for the next step…

Put the remaining 1 cup of blueberries and 2 tablespoons of sugar into a small saucepan, and turn the heat up to medium high. Cook, stirring regularly, until the blueberries have mostly turned to liquid. Spoon the blueberry liquid onto the muffins, dividing it more or less evenly. Use a toothpick to give each muffin a quick swirl, incorporating some of the liquid into the muffin.

Mix the lemon zest and turbinado sugar together, and sprinkle over the muffins. Bake for 18 minutes, or until a toothpick inserted into the middle of a muffin (that miraculously manages to miss a blueberry) comes out clean.

As soon as the muffins come out of the oven, use a butter knife to gently loosen any muffins whose topping has spilled over onto the tin – otherwise the topping will glue them down firmly as it cools. Then wait 5 minutes before teasing them out of the tins with a pair of forks (one slides down the side, the other then scoops up from underneath) – if you try this too soon, the muffins won't be quite as sturdy, and some crushing is likely to occur.

Done! It was worth it, as you shall see…

Notes:

> These are the *relaxed* directions – they assume that you are in no great rush. If that is not the case, preheat your oven sooner than I say, and start the topping cooking on the stove before you add the wet ingredients to the dry. You will have to stir the topping and keep an eye on it while you finish making the muffins and filling the cups, which is entirely possible, and certainly quicker, but adds a little stress to the process. In particular it makes the timing slightly tricky – if the topping is ready too quickly, it will thicken and be harder to work with. But if it's a busy day, or you simply abhor inefficiency, go for it.
>
> If your blueberries are not sufficiently juicy, then you can cook them forever and they will never turn to liquid. This is rarely the case, but it can happen. If it does, oh well, fake it – they will still be good. (Or check your blueberries before starting, and if they're not reasonably juicy, bail.)
>
> Don't mix the lemon zest and turbinado sugar until the moment you're ready to sprinkle them on the muffins – if left to sit they turn into a paste that is difficult to work with.
>
> If you don't have buttermilk, use 1 tablespoon of lemon juice or white vinegar topped up with milk to make a cup.

Pumpkin Chocolate Chip Muffins

These are always popular. One can of pumpkin makes two dozen muffins, which is nice (more is better…).

Yield: 24 muffins.

    3 1/4 C flour (390 g)
    2 C sugar
    2 tsps baking powder
    2 tsps baking soda
    1 tsp cinnamon
    1 tsp salt
    1 (15 oz) can pumpkin
    4 eggs
    1 C oil
    2 C semisweet chocolate chips

Preheat the oven to 400°, without convection, with a rack in the middle or just above. Line two muffin tins with paper muffin cups.

Mix the dry ingredients and wet ingredients in separate bowls, then add the wet to the dry, along with the chocolate chips, and combine just until uniform. Spoon into the muffin cups, and bake for 15 – 20 minutes, until a toothpick comes out clean. Let sit for 5 minutes before removing to wire racks to cool.

Corn Bread
Adapted from "Moosewood Cookbook" by Mollie Katzen.

1 C cornmeal
1 C flour
2 tsps baking powder
1/2 tsp baking soda
1/2 tsp salt
1 C buttermilk
2 eggs
1/4 C honey
3 or 4 Tbs melted butter

Preheat the oven to 400°, without convection, with a rack in the middle or just above. Line the bottom of a 9 inch round cake pan with a piece of parchment paper, and grease the sides of the pan.

Mix the dry ingredients together in a large bowl, and mix the buttermilk, eggs, and honey together in a small bowl. Add the wet ingredients to the dry, along with the melted butter, and stir until well combined. Transfer to the cake pan, and bake for about 20 minutes.

Let cool for a few minutes before loosening the sides and removing from the pan.

Serve warm, ideally with raspberry jam.

Notes:

> The baking is a little persnickety – too long, and it will be dry; not long enough, and it will be uncooked in the middle. A 9 inch round cake pan really is the best bet for pulling this off, but if you don't have one, a 9 inch pie tin can work, as can an 8 inch square cake pan.
>
> If you have no buttermilk, you can use a mixture of half yogurt and half milk. Or, in a pinch, you can add milk to one tablespoon of lemon juice or white vinegar until you have one cup.
>
> For a nice variation, add a cup of corn kernels to the batter (if they're frozen, defrost them first – room temperature is ideal).
>
> To make these into a dozen muffins, spoon into muffin cups and bake at 375°, with convection, for about 15 minutes.

Aunt Sue's Irish Soda Bread

The best. You might think the caraway seeds are strange (and I've seen some recipes that leave them out); they are *essential* and excellent.

Since two loaves fit on a large cookie sheet, I always make two at a time (and slice and freeze one); you can certainly halve the recipe and make only one, if you prefer.

Yield: 2 round loaves.

> 555 g flour (4 1/2 C plus 2 Tbs)
> 1 Tbs baking powder
> 1 1/2 tsps baking soda
> 2 tsps salt
> 3/8 C sugar (1/4 C plus 2 Tbs)
> 1 Tbs caraway seeds
> 6 Tbs butter (plus a little extra, for brushing, and for greasing the pan)
> 2 C buttermilk
> 1 1/3 C raisins
> 1 – 1 1/2 Tbs turbinado sugar

Preheat the oven to 350°, without convection, with a rack in the middle, or just above. Grease a large cookie sheet or half sheet pan.

Mix together the flour, baking powder, baking soda, salt, sugar, and caraway seeds. Cut in the butter, as finely as you have patience for – no more. Stir in the buttermilk and the raisins. Turn the dough onto a floured surface and briefly knead, just a few strokes, to complete the mixing. (It will be quite moist and sticky.) Divide in two, shape each half into a round, and space them evenly on the cookie sheet. Cut the loaves crosswise into quarters, about 2/3 of the way through (washing the knife frequently helps). Brush with melted butter and sprinkle generously with turbinado sugar, then bake until lightly browned, about 35 – 40 minutes.

Date Nut Bread

This is adapted from a recipe that's been floating around the internet, and may have originated with the *Old Farmer's Almanac*. Moist, rich, and exceptionally delicious.

Yield: 1 loaf.

    1 C boiling coffee
    1 tsp baking soda
    8 oz whole pitted dates, sliced in half
    a little less than 1 C sugar
    1 Tbs butter, melted
    1 egg
    a pinch of salt
    1 tsp vanilla
    1 1/2 C flour
    1 heaping C very coarsely chopped walnuts

Pour the boiling coffee over the dates and stir in the baking soda; set aside.

Preheat the oven to 300°, without convection, with a rack in the middle or just below.

Mix together the sugar, melted butter, egg, salt, and vanilla until smooth. Add the flour and walnuts, mix briefly, then pour in the date mixture and mix well.

Transfer to a greased loaf pan, and bake for about 1 1/4 to 1 1/2 hours, until a toothpick comes out clean.

Cool for 10 minutes in the pan, then remove to cool on a rack.

Notes:

    Measure the coffee after it boils – if you measure it first and then boil it, some of it boils off and you end up with less than 1 cup.

    Cutting the dates in half ensures that no stray pits go undetected.

    I usually triple the recipe and freeze a couple of loaves, sliced.

Banana Chocolate Chip Scones

You need something to do with overripe bananas; this is it. Delicious. You'll never make banana bread again.

Yield: 12 scones.

    3 C flour
    1/2 C brown sugar, packed
    2 tsps baking powder
    1/4 tsp baking soda
    1/2 tsp salt
    3 Tbs butter
    3 overripe bananas, mashed (between 1 and 1 1/2 cups)
    1/4 C buttermilk
    2 egg whites
    1 tsp vanilla
    1/2 C semisweet chocolate chips
    1 – 2 Tbs turbinado sugar

Preheat the oven to 400°, without convection, with a shelf in the middle or just below.

Mix the dry ingredients together in a large bowl (since brown sugar is usually somewhat lumpy, this is best done by rubbing the ingredients between your palms). Cut in the butter until it is in very small pieces.

Mix together the mashed bananas, egg whites, buttermilk, and vanilla. Add the wet ingredients to the dry, add the chocolate chips, and stir just until the batter is mostly uniform. Turn out onto a floured surface and knead a few strokes, then transfer to a large greased cookie sheet. Press the dough into a 9 inch diameter circle.

Use a dough knife (a.k.a. bench scraper, or just a knife) to cut the dough into twelve equal slices. Keep the knife clean and slightly damp (otherwise it will stick in the dough), and use it to separate the slices a little on the baking tray – give it a little side-to-side twist at the end of each cut.

Bake for 20 minutes, until lightly browned. Let cool a few minutes before sliding the whole thing onto a rack to cool. Use a knife to separate the scones just before serving.

Bread

General Instructions

There is much to be said about bread, and if I try to say all I should, I'll end up with a second book. So instead I will provide just a few notes and thoughts, and trust that you will pick up the rest elsewhere.

Probably the most important thing to understand is that yeast is a living organism. We buy it dried and dormant; water revives it. It is most active in warm temperatures; hot temperatures will kill it, and it gets sluggish in cool temperatures, eventually returning to dormancy when it gets too cold. It should be stored in the refrigerator or freezer, carefully protected from moisture.

The beauty of yeast is that as it consumes some of the sugars and starches in the dough, it gives off carbon dioxide, which accumulates into bubbles, causing the dough to expand and rise. How much the dough rises is a complicated function of how much yeast you use, how warm it is, how much time you give it, and the composition of the dough itself. There is a great deal of flexibility, and good results can be achieved with a wide range of techniques. I generally rise my doughs for a total of about 4 hours before baking, but you can rush that a bit if necessary (use a little more yeast and keep the dough quite warm), or drag it out to accommodate your schedule (less yeast, cooler temperatures – some rising occurs even in the refrigerator). You can experiment – the worst that can happen is the bread might not turn out quite like you wanted. It will still be good.

In addition to carbon dioxide, yeast gives off other by-products (famously including alcohol) which add flavor to the dough. These are most prominent in doughs that rise a long time (sourdough breads, for an extreme example), and for this reason, as well as some added structure, we sometimes "pre-ferment" a portion of the dough. This is basically done by preparing part of the dough the night before, and combining that with the "fresh" dough the next day. There are a number of techniques; I am partial to "poolish" because it gives good results and is the easiest to make. There are instructions in the recipes that use it, but the idea is to add a tiny bit of yeast to some water (it doesn't have to be too warm) and mix in flour to a spongy consistency. It can be done with a wooden spoon, and just takes a minute. The next day it will be a lovely mass of craters and bubbles, with a great smell.

And then there is the flour. Wheat flour, to be precise, because of its gluten content. This provides the structure that holds the bread up, letting it rise vertically instead of collapsing. Gluten is made up of proteins that can be coerced into bonding together to form long strands – this is what kneading seeks to accomplish (whether by hand or using a stand mixer with a dough hook). We encourage the development of the gluten by mixing and kneading smoothly and always in the same direction, and avoiding actions that cut into the dough as much as possible.

"Folding" the dough partway through rising further develops the gluten; this is just a matter of turning the dough out onto a floured surface, and essentially giving it a few gentle kneading strokes – fold it in half, press down, give it a quarter turn, and repeat a few times. This also lets some of the air out of the dough, which seems counterproductive, but actually reinvigorates the yeast and encourages more complete rising.

And speaking of rising, even if your house is warm, countertops can be cold in the winter – especially if they're stone and over cabinets against an exterior wall. Bagels and bialys in particular do better rising on a wooden table. If that's inconvenient, try insulating them from the countertop with a wooden cutting board.

After baking, bread should be promptly removed from loaf pans and left to cool on wire racks. The cooler the bread is before slicing the better; fend off those who want it cut prematurely for as long as you can, and then surrender with grace.

Unlike wine, and me, bread doesn't get better with age, and rather than leave them to get stale on the counter, I generally slice and freeze my breads the day I make them. You can make a sandwich in the morning on frozen bread, and by the time you're ready for lunch it will be completely defrosted and ready to eat. And if you can't wait for lunch, it's always good toasted.

Below: Poolish.

Challah

You can make one very large, impressive challah out of this recipe, or else you can make three sandwich-sized breads in loaf pans.

    1 3/4 C warm water (414 g)
    3 tsps yeast
    7 eggs (one for brushing)
    1/2 C oil
    1/4 C sugar
    2 3/4 tsps salt
    about 9 C flour (1080 g)

Dissolve the yeast in the water, and warm six of the eggs in a large bowl of hot tap water.

Mix four of the warmed eggs and the yolks of the two others with the oil, sugar, and salt (the remaining two egg whites are not used). Measure about seven cups of flour into a large mixing bowl, and form a deep well in the center. Pour in the egg mixture, and stir to incorporate some of the flour into the eggs. Add the water and yeast, and continue stirring until all of the flour is mixed in. Knead in the remaining flour until the dough is smooth, not stiff, and a little sticky. Place in a bowl, cover with plastic, and let rise for an hour and a half.

For one large loaf, I am a fan of the 6-strand braid. For that, divide the dough into six more or less equal pieces, and roll each one into a rope 2 to 3 feet long. (Longer is better, if you have the room to work, as it makes a more intricate braid. As for rolling out the strands, it helps to do this in stages – roll each piece partway, then start over and roll each one a bit longer, and so on. This lets them relax and loosen up a bit, so they stretch more readily. Be very frugal with the flour you use on the surface – a little stickiness aids the process.) Follow the 6-strand braid instructions on the next page. I strongly recommend practicing on some rope first… Once the loaf is braided, lay *two* sheets of parchment paper in your largest cookie sheet, so that they overlap and in particular completely cover two opposite corners. (It is possible to simply grease the cookie sheet, but the egg wash you will be using bakes into an effective glue, and if you go this route you can expect some unpleasantness liberating the bread from the pan.) Starting at one end of the loaf, snake one arm underneath as far as you can, and then do what you can with the other to lift the bread and maneuver it onto the cookie sheet diagonally, aligning the ends with the excess of parchment paper. Some distorting will occur; no matter, you can even it out once you have it settled in place.

For three loaves, divide the dough in thirds, then divide each third further into thirds, and braid "normally." Fit these into greased (or parchment paper lined) loaf pans.

Beat the remaining egg, and brush it all over the loaf (or loaves). Reserve the leftover egg – you will brush the challah again before it goes in the oven. Let rise another hour and a half. (Do not try to cover the bread – anything you use will stick horribly.)

Preheat the oven to 350°, without convection, with a shelf just below the middle. Just before baking, brush the loaves again with the remaining egg. For three smaller loaves, bake for 30 minutes. For one large loaf, bake for 35 minutes.

Note: The amount of flour is approximate because there is some variation even in eggs of the same nominal size. As mentioned elsewhere, I use "extra large" eggs; if yours are larger or smaller, you will need to adjust the amount of flour accordingly.

6-Strand Braid:

Arrange your six strands into two groups of three, and make a triangle with you at the base, three strands to the left, three to the right, and all six meeting at the point, farthest from you. Pinch the strands together where they meet.

Number the strands 1 – 6, left to right. You should have 1, 2, and 3 angling down to your left, and 4, 5, and 6 angling down to your right.

There is a single starting step, and then once that is done, a pattern that repeats until the braid is complete. We will only use the numbers for the starting step. Which is this: Lift 4, then pass 1 over 2 and 3, under 4, and over 5 and 6 – so that it ends up pointing off to the right – and lower 4 back to where it was. The only strand that has really moved in this step is 1; the others are where they were, and 1 is no longer part of the "triangle" – it points right.

You now have two strands on your left, and on your right you have three more-or-less parallel strands, and a fourth crossing them and pointing off to the side. This is the "right-heavy" arrangement; our next maneuver will change it to "left-heavy," and the braiding will be a matter of alternating between these two configurations. Take the outermost of the three parallel strands on the right and swing it left, over and across the other two right strands and the two left strands, so that it points to the far left. Then "follow" it with the strand that points far right, laying this strand parallel to the two left strands, on the innermost (right) side of them.

You now have four strands on the left: one points off to the left side, the other three are parallel (the rightmost of these is the one that used to be pointing off to the far right). Two strands remain on the right; the situation is now "left-heavy." So lift the outermost of the three parallel left strands, and bring it right, across the other two left and the two right strands, and leave it pointing right. Follow it with the strand pointing left, making it the new inner (leftmost) strand on the right.

And now the braid is "right-heavy"… Repeat, and repeat, and repeat…

When you get down to where the strands are too short to braid, fuse together the last bits and tuck them under a little to clean up.

I highly recommend making one of these to practice with, before you try to braid dough – it's much more forgiving of mistakes:

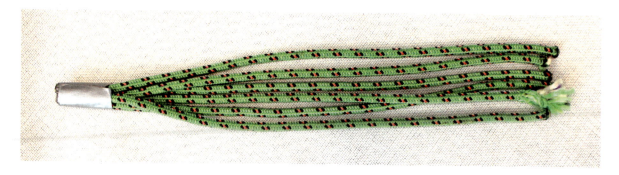

Bagels

The best. Unless you live near one of the finest New York bagel bakeries – and maybe even if you do – you will never be satisfied with a commercial bagel again. Sorry.

Yield: 12 bagels.

Dough:

>650 g warm water (about 2 3/4 C)
>1 tsp yeast
>1 1/2 Tbs sugar
>1 Tbs barley malt syrup
>3 1/2 tsps salt
>1050 g bread flour

Toppings:

>Dried minced onion, dried minced garlic, sesame seeds, poppy seeds, coarse salt.

Boiling:

>6 quarts water
>2 Tbs malt extract
>1 tsp salt

Sprinkle the yeast over the water in the bowl of a stand mixer; add the sugar and malt, and stir briefly to combine. Add roughly 2/3 of the flour and then the salt, and process for half a minute or so with the mixing attachment. Add most of the remaining flour (reserve a tiny bit – maybe two teaspoons – for dusting the work surface), and process with the dough hook until the dough is well kneaded and smooth. Use the reserved flour to finish kneading the dough briefly by hand. Cover with plastic and let rest for 15 minutes.

Working on an unfloured surface, divide the dough into 12 equal pieces, by weight (weigh the dough and divide; you should find them to be about 145 grams each). Work each piece into a rough ball (by folding and turning repeatedly, as if kneading, and then gathering opposite sides up together to finish), and set aside on a dishtowel; cover with another dishtowel followed by plastic wrap, for another 15 minute rest.

Form each ball into a bagel by pinching a hole in the middle and gently stretching into a ring shape. The hole will fill in somewhat during rising and baking, and must therefore be larger than you might think – a 4 1/2 inch diameter ring with a 2 – 2 1/2 inch diameter hole is about right. (At this stage they don't have to be pretty – they will round themselves out in the oven.) Set the shaped bagels back on the dishtowel, cover again with a dishtowel and plastic, and let rise for 2 hours.

Half an hour before the bagels are finished rising, start the boiling liquid heating in your largest pot, and preheat the oven to 450°, with convection, with a rack in the lower middle.

Arrange your toppings in small bowls, and lay out a clean dishtowel next to a large cookie sheet. When the bagels are ready, drop three at a time into the boiling water. They will quickly float to the top. Boil for one minute, turning them over halfway through, then remove with a slotted spoon or wire strainer and place them on the dishtowel. Sprinkle with toppings, turn over, and sprinkle the other sides. Transfer the bagels to the cookie sheet, and boil the next three. Once you have six ready, load them into the oven and bake for about 13 minutes, until golden brown.

Notes:

All purpose flour will not do; bagels require the higher gluten content of bread flour.

The recipe makes bagels that are a little larger than their commercial counterparts; I think this is a plus, and since you can fit 6 in the oven at a time regardless, it's even more efficient. But if you'd prefer your bagels a little smaller, decrease the flour, water, and salt by 5 – 10 percent (3 1/2 teaspoons of salt weighs about 24 grams). You can just skimp slightly on the yeast, sugar, and malt, and it will be fine (but if you feel the need to be more precise about it, be my guest).

You can of course make these by hand, without a stand mixer, but bagel dough is quite stiff, and you will get a good workout kneading. Don't give up – get all the flour in there…

"Barley malt syrup" is also known as "malt extract" or "malted barley extract." If you can't find it at the supermarket, homebrew suppliers sell it (if you buy it from a homebrew supplier, make sure you buy the *unhopped* variety — hops is very nice in beer; not so nice in bagels…). If you store it in the refrigerator (as some manufacturers suggest), warm the jar (without the lid!) briefly in the microwave before adding it to the dough. (Or, if you have the foresight, take it out the night before so that it's at room temperature when you use it.)

When shaping the dough into balls and then bagels ("tori," to be precise about the shape name), if you lay the dish towel you're using in a cookie sheet, then you'll be able to relocate the bagels easily. You can get a dozen balls of bagel dough onto one dishtowel in a cookie sheet, but once you finish shaping them, only six (so you'll need two towels, two cookie sheets, plus the two dishtowels for covers, not to mention the one for the toppings – it's a towel-intensive operation…).

I use convection because my oven holds its temperature better when I do, especially for such a short cooking time. But they bake fine without it (same temperature).

Making two dozen bagels is not twice as much work as one. You'll have to do two passes through the stand mixer, but the 15 minute rests correspond nicely to the amount of time needed to assemble (the first rest) and divide (the second rest) the second batch. You don't need to increase the boiling liquid; there will be plenty. If you try to make more than two dozen, I hope you have assistance…

If, for some strange reason, you care to make plain, seedless bagels, then make sure to line your baking sheets with parchment paper, or they will stick quite miserably.

If you do some research you will find that commercially made bagels are shaped and then refrigerated overnight before baking. The claim is that this improves the flavor; I went to quite a bit of trouble to test this and could not discern any difference. My strong suspicion is that the primary motivation behind the commercial method is expediency – if you need many dozens of bagels to be ready at 6:00 in the morning, you'd better have formed them the night before, so you can start boiling and baking them as soon as you get in.

Hy's Amazing Bagel Crackers

You've just made bagels (good for you), and now you have a big pile of beautiful seeds that you can't save (because they're damp from the wet bagels), and a big pot of beautiful bagel water. So you make these crackers. It turns out that they're the best crackers ever, bar none. Amazing.

    about 3/4 C leftover bagel seeds
2 C (all purpose) flour
1/2 tsp baking powder
1/2 C water used to boil bagels (hot is fine)
1/4 C oil

Preheat the oven to 425°, with convection, with a rack in the upper middle.

Mix together the flour, seeds, and baking powder. Mix together the water and oil (which is impossible, but that's okay…), then add to the flour mixture. Combine, ultimately mixing with your hands, to form a dough. Divide in half.

Roll half the dough out on a lightly floured surface as thinly as the seeds will permit, about 1/16 of an inch. Cut into crackers with a pizza cutter, bench scraper, or knife, and arrange on an ungreased cookie sheet, as close together as possible – fitting each half of the dough on one cookie sheet can be challenging. Bake for 7 – 12 minutes, until lightly browned; cool on racks.

Repeat with the rest of the dough.

Notes:

    The crackers get their salt from the salt that doesn't stick when topping the bagels, so if you don't use salt as a topping, you'll need to add some. On the other hand, if you use a lot of salt on your bagels, and much of it doesn't stick, then the crackers will be salty. Keep it in mind when you're making your bagels. I find that making salt the first topping I sprinkle on the bagels, so that most of it sticks, does the trick.

    If you use garlic as a topping, be very careful not to overcook the crackers – the garlic becomes unpleasantly bitter if it burns.

    The wide range of cooking times reflects the crackers' sensitivity to oven temperature. Watch them carefully after they've been in for a little while; they brown quickly.

Bialys

If there's a bialy recipe out there somewhere, the chances are excellent that I've looked at it. This recipe is the result of that research, along with a great deal of experimentation and revision. I think I've pretty much nailed it…

Yield: 18 bialys.

Dough:

> 667 g warm water (about 2 3/4 C)
> 4 g yeast
> 25 g salt
> 1024 g bread flour

Filling:

> 1 medium onion
> 1 Tbs unseasoned white bread crumbs or matzoh meal
> 1 or 2 tsps poppy seeds, optional

Put the water in the bowl of a stand mixer, sprinkle on the yeast, and allow to sit a minute or two for the yeast to dissolve before stirring briefly with a fork. Add roughly 2/3 of the flour, then the salt, and mix with the stand mixer's mixing attachment. Then add most of the remaining flour (reserve a tablespoon or two), switch to the dough hook, and mix for a few minutes. Dust the reserved flour onto a clean surface and knead briefly by hand. Place the dough in a large (ungreased) mixing bowl, cover with plastic wrap, and let rise for 2 or 3 hours, folding halfway through.

While the dough rises, prepare the filling. Coarsely chop the onions, and then pulse them in a food processor until they are finely minced. Drain them briefly in a wire strainer, pressing out some of the liquid, before combining with the bread crumbs or matzoh meal (to further absorb liquid) and optional poppy seeds. Alternately, you can mince the onions by hand, but they will release less liquid, and the final product is less likely to have the characteristic pink tinge of a truly authentic bialy. (But they will still be good.)

When the dough is ready, divide it into 18 even portions (by weight; some arithmetic is required). Form each of these into a tight ball by kneading a little, then repeatedly stretching up opposite sides to meet in the middle and pinching closed (stop before the surface begins to tear). Place the balls seam side down 2 inches apart on a clean dish towel. Cover with a second dish towel, cover that with plastic wrap, and let rise 1 1/2 hours. (If the plastic wrap lies directly on the bialys, it sticks. And if there's no plastic wrap over the top towel, the dough dries out on top.)

Place a baking stone on a rack in the lower third of the oven. About 45 minutes before the dough is done with this final rise, preheat the oven to 500° (*without* convection – the ones in the front of the oven brown too quickly with convection).

Place a sheet of parchment paper on a pizza peel (the bialys will bake – 6 at a time – on the parchment paper directly on the baking stone). The paper should be oriented so its longer dimension lies across the peel from left to right, to facilitate sliding it onto the stone with a forward motion.

Lightly flour a work surface. To form a bialy, lay a ball on the work surface, and begin by pressing both thumbs firmly down in the center to start the depression. Then lift the dough up and hold it vertically, supported by your thumbs on the inside. Turn the dough, pinching and stretching, to widen the bialy, until it is about 5 inches in diameter, with a center depression of about 3 to 3 1/2 inches. (As the bialys rise in the oven, the sides will expand and fill in the center, so these have to be *much* wider than you might imagine in order to get a reasonably proportioned end result. In particular, the center depression should appear much too wide before baking.)

As you complete each bialy, place it onto the parchment paper on the pizza peel, leaving what room you can spare between neighbors (it won't be much, but that doesn't matter – they rise *up*

more than they expand side to side, and if they end up touching a little, it's okay), until you have 6 of them done. Spread about a teaspoon of filling in the center of each, and slide the parchment paper off the peel and onto the baking stone. Turn the oven down to 480°, and bake for 9 – 11 minutes, until well browned all over. When they are done, use the pizza peel to remove the bialys from the oven; this is a tricky feat requiring extraordinary balance and a little luck… You'll see. (If you drop one on the floor, pick it up quickly and don't tell anybody.)

Slide the parchment paper out from under the cooked bialys and cool on a wire rack. Return the oven to 500° and repeat the process for the next batch.

Notes:

You really do have to use *bread* flour – all purpose flour won't do. (Bread flour has more gluten, which gives the bialys their consistency.)

Opening the oven loses heat; preheating to 500° makes it more likely that they actually cook at 480° from the beginning.

It helps to have two peels, so that you can prepare a batch on one while reserving the other to remove the batch that's in the oven. And it's easier if the one used to remove the bialys from the oven is metal – the metal ones are thinner, and slide under the parchment paper easily.

Khachapuri Rolls
Inspired by the "Mingrelian Khachapuri" recipe at foodperestroika.com.

"Mingrelian Khachapuri" is a cheese-filled bread the point of which seems to be to determine how much fat one can consume without dying, or at least wanting to die. It's delicious; I could only manage one bite.

These rolls are my attempt to scale the original back to something you can confess to your cardiologist. It has far more butter than I would normally condone, but given it's origins, I think it's okay. And it remains absolutely delicious.

Start these 4 to 4 1/2 hours before dinner.

Yield: 12 rolls.

Dough:

>160 g milk (about 5/8 C)
>340 g yogurt (about 1 1/4 C)
>1 stick (1/2 C) butter, melted
>1 egg, lightly beaten
>10 g sugar
>8 g salt
>10 g yeast
>600 g bread flour

Filling:

>200 g fresh mozzarella
>100 g feta packed in brine (drained)
>1/8 tsp salt

Glaze:

>1 egg, lightly beaten

Warm the milk and yogurt briefly in the microwave, then combine the milk, yogurt, melted butter, beaten egg, sugar, and salt in the bowl of a stand mixer. Mix briefly with the paddle attachment. Make sure it's not too warm, then sprinkle in the yeast, let sit a moment, and mix it in. Add the flour and mix with the paddle attachment for a few minutes, until a smooth but quite sticky dough forms. Cover with plastic wrap, and let rise for 1 1/2 hours.

Lightly punch down the dough, and let rise for another 1 to 1 1/2 hours.

While the dough is rising, mix the filling ingredients together until uniform (a food processor works well, but it is also possible to just use your fingers…).

Preheat the oven to 400°, without convection, with a baking stone (or steel) on a rack in the middle or just below. Line a large baking sheet with parchment paper (or lightly oil it).

On a lightly floured surface, divide the dough into 12 equal portions (they should be about 104 g each), and form into roughly circular disks (they need not be spherical – you are about to flatten them). Press a disk into a 4 inch diameter circle with your palm and fingers; it should be thinner at the edges than in the middle. Take 24 g (about 1 tablespoon) of the filling, roll it into a ball, and place it in the center of the flattened dough. Gather up the edges and pinch them together around the filling, like closing a drawstring purse. Place the roll seam side down on the prepared baking tray, and repeat with the remaining dough pieces.

Brush each roll lightly with the beaten egg, and poke a hole in the top with a chopstick or something similar, making sure to get all the way down to the cheese. Wiggle the chopstick around a bit to widen the opening – the cheese wants out, and unless you provide an avenue for steam to escape, it will certainly find its way. Bake for 15 – 20 minutes, until well browned on top; serve warm.

Notes:

In keeping with the goal of maximizing the fat content, the original recipe calls for whole milk and full fat yogurt. I use 1% milk and lowfat yogurt; whatever you have around will be fine.

An alternative to poking a hole in the top of each roll is to place them on the baking tray seam side *up*. This looks a little messy at first, but it evens out pretty well in the oven, and might even be more effective in keeping the cheese from bursting through the rolls. (Neither method is foolproof though, and you can expect to lose a few. They will still be delicious.)

Dinner or Burger Rolls

Homemade rolls make all the difference. Start these about 3 1/2 hours before dinner.

Yield: 12 dinner rolls or 8 burger rolls.

> 1 C warm milk
> 2 tsps yeast
> 1 egg, warmed in a bowl of hot tap water
> 2 Tbs sugar
> 1/4 C oil
> 1 tsp salt
> 3 1/2 C flour (420 g)

Dissolve the yeast in the milk, then combine with the remaining ingredients in the bowl of a stand mixer (or a mixing bowl, if kneading by hand), reserving 2 or 3 tablespoons of flour to finish kneading by hand. The resulting dough should be smooth, soft, and somewhat sticky. Set aside to rise in a lightly oiled bowl for 1 1/2 hours.

Punch down, divide into 12 pieces for dinner rolls or 8 pieces for burger rolls, and form into balls. For dinner rolls, place these about 1/2 inch apart on an oiled 8 × 12 × 2 inch baking tray. Burger rolls can either be baked in the same size tray, in which case they will be tall and not so wide, or else on an oiled cookie sheet, about an inch apart, to give them some room to spread. Cover with a dry towel, and then a sheet of plastic wrap, and let rise for about 45 minutes (you can adjust the time a bit so that they come out of the oven 15 – 20 minutes before dinner).

Bake in a preheated 350° oven, in the middle or just above, without convection, for 20 – 25 minutes.

Notes:

> You can easily double the recipe (and either use two 8 × 12 × 2 inch trays or one half sheet pan or large cookie sheet), but they don't keep especially well, so it's best to make only as much as you'll consume fresh from the oven.
>
> Some people like to spread these with butter as they come out of the oven. If that sounds good to you, just rub a stick of butter over the tops of the hot rolls – no need to melt it first.

French Bread Baguettes

Yield: 4 large or 6 small baguettes.

Poolish:

>473 g warm water (2 C)
1/8 tsp yeast
450 g C flour (3 3/4 C)

Add:

>237 g warm water (1 C)
1 1/2 tsps yeast
690 g flour (5 3/4 C)
1 Tbs plus 1/4 tsp salt

For baking:

>water
semolina

Make the poolish the night before: Dissolve the yeast in the water, add the flour, and mix briefly with a wooden spoon to form a rough dough. Cover, and let sit overnight.

To finish the dough, dissolve the remaining yeast in the remaining water in the bowl of a stand mixer (or mixing bowl, if you are making the breads by hand), add about 2 cups of flour, then the salt, and mix with the paddle attachment (or a wooden spoon). Add the poolish, and continue mixing until it has been well incorporated. Switch to the dough hook, add most of the remaining flour (reserve 2 or 3 tablespoons), and mix or knead well. Use the reserved flour to finish kneading the dough by hand; it should be well developed but still noticeably moist when finished.

Let rise for 1 1/2 hours, fold, then rise for another 1 hour.

Divide the dough into 4 or 6 equal pieces. (In either case, you will have to bake them in two batches. It is a little easier to load 3 small baguettes on a pizza peel lengthwise and slide them onto a baking stone than it is to load 2 larger baguettes diagonally. With a little practice, though, you should be able to handle the larger baguettes without too much trouble – you might occasionally get one that isn't quite straight, but that is not a disaster.)

Form each piece into a baguette… This is not difficult, but the technique takes a little explaining, so here goes: On a floured surface, fold the top third of the dough over, rotate it 180°, and then do the same. (The shape of the dough when you start is of no consequence whatsoever – it can be uneven and disfigured, and have bits stuck on from when you adjusted the pieces to have the same weight.) Assuming you are right handed (make the obvious changes if not), starting on the right side of the dough, lay your left thumb along the length of the dough, and use the fingers of your right hand to fold the dough over your thumb and compress it. Then slide your thumb a little to the left, and repeat, working your way down the length of the dough in this manner until you reach the left end. This creates a "seam" along the top of the dough; keeping the seam side up, rotate the dough 180° again, and once again start on the right and work your way to the left, folding the dough over your left thumb with your right fingers. As you continue to repeat this process, the dough will naturally elongate into a baguette shape – long and thin, tightly compressed, and essentially equal in diameter throughout. Stop when the dough is an appropriate length for your peel and stone (based on whether you are making 4 or 6 loaves).

Arrange the loaves seam-side up on kitchen towels, making sure they don't touch (pull up the towel to form a barrier between loaves), cover with a towel as well, and with plastic wrap over that. Let rise for 1 1/2 hours.

At least 45 minutes before the breads are done rising, place a baking stone on a shelf below the center of the oven and a shallow pan (such as a broiling pan) on the floor of the oven, and preheat the oven to 460°, without convection. (The pan on the floor of the oven will receive boiling water, to steam the oven.)

When it is time to bake the breads, start 1/2 cup of water heating in a frying pan, and dust a pizza peel lightly with semolina. To transfer a baguette to the peel, lift under the towel with one hand and flip the baguette onto your other (floured) arm, so that your arm supports its entire length. Arrange the baguettes on the peel with as much space between them as you can manage, either with 3 baguettes lying the length of the peel, or 2 lying diagonally (if you're right handed, they should go from the far left corner to the near right corner, where "near" means close to the handle – this will make it easiest to slide them onto the stone with your right hand). You can scrunch them up a bit, lengthwise, if they go past the ends of the peel.

With a very sharp knife, cut diagonal slits across the tops of the baguettes, an inch or two apart. It's traditional to angle the knife a bit, so that you are cutting something of a flap. In any case, these give the breads room to rise, and if they are not deep enough or spaced too far apart, then your bread will suffer accordingly. Half an inch, on an angle, is about right.

When the water is boiling, quickly (and carefully!) pour it into the pan on the oven floor, then load the breads onto the stone. Immediately start another 1/2 cup of water boiling, and as soon as it is ready, pour it, too, into the pan on the oven floor. Bake the breads for about 15 – 18 minutes, until they are richly colored.

Note: There are undoubtedly many reasonable ways to form baguettes; the method I describe is adapted from Jeffrey Hamelman's *Bread: A Baker's Book of Techniques and Recipes* (remarkable for being a 400 page book on bread making that, as far as I can tell, never uses the word "knead" even once. A good book nonetheless.)

Hy's Best Sandwich Bread

This is a multigrain bread; nutritious and delicious. The millet provides a nice crunch, but requires soaking in boiling water (otherwise the crunch is of the dental emergency kind). This sets the whole process back a couple of hours, waiting for the grains to cool, but it's worth it.

Because the dough is fairly moist, it's a bit unpleasant to knead by hand – a stand mixer makes the job easier, and the instructions below assume that you'll use one. But if you don't, don't worry – just ignore the bits about attachments…

Three loaves is the most my mixer can handle, and also fits nicely in the oven without crowding, but the recipe can easily be scaled up or down.

Yield: 3 loaves.

> 860 g boiling water (3 3/4 C)
> 1 1/2 C rolled oats
> 3/4 C millet
> 3 Tbs ground flax seed meal
> 174 g warm water (3/4 C)
> 2 1/4 tsps yeast
> 4 1/2 tsps salt
> 1080 g flour (9 C)
> about 3 Tbs butter

Put the oats, millet, and flax seed meal in the bowl of a stand mixer (or a large mixing bowl), pour the boiling water over the grains, and mix briefly. Leave this to sit for a couple of hours, stirring occasionally, until the mixture is just warm throughout – cool enough to pose no danger to the yeast.

Add the yeast to the warm water, stir to dissolve, and pour into the bowl with the grains. Mix this briefly with a wooden spoon. Add about 2/3 of the flour, then the salt, and mix using the paddle (mixing) attachment for a minute or two. (The point here is to get the bulk of the ingredients well mixed; the dough hook does a good job kneading, but a lousy job mixing…)

Switch to the dough hook, add most of the remaining flour (reserve a tablespoon or two), and process for a few minutes. You may need to reposition the dough on the hook once or twice to ensure even kneading. Spread the remaining bit of flour on a clean surface, and finish by kneading the dough by hand for a few turns. The dough should be moist but not overly sticky.

Put the dough in a large mixing bowl, cover with plastic wrap, and let rise for 3 hours, folding after 1 1/2 hours.

Butter three loaf pans. Divide the dough evenly into three pieces, form each into a tight loaf, and place these in the pans. Cover with plastic wrap, and let rise 1 hour.

Before the breads are finished rising in their pans, preheat the oven to 400°, without convection, with a rack just below the middle. Shortly before the hour is up, melt about 2 tablespoons of butter.

Slit the tops of the loaves about 3/4 of an inch deep, and brush generously with the melted butter. Bake for 30 minutes, switching the positions of the two outer loaves (and leaving the one in the middle where it is) after 20 minutes, to promote even baking.

As soon as the loaves are done, remove them from the pans and cool on wire racks.

Note: The density of water decreases with increased temperature, so a cup of boiling water weighs less than a cup of warm water, which weighs less than a cup of cool water. For this reason, the weights specified in the recipe for the boiling and warm water won't seem to agree with published weights for water (about 237 g per cup). I measured these quantities, rather than calculated them, so they may not precisely correspond to the specified volumes at the temperatures of boiling and "warm" water, but if you weigh your water, that won't matter.

Also, weigh the boiling water *after* boiling it – if you weigh it first, some of it is lost as steam. Be careful…

Sunflower Bread
Inspired by a recipe in Jeffrey Hamelman's "Bread."

Yield: 2 loaves.

Poolish:

    355 g lukewarm water (1 1/2 C)
    1/8 tsp yeast
    360 g flour (3 C)

Dough:

    2 C raw sunflower seeds
    355 g warm water (1 1/2 C)
    1 Tbs barley malt syrup
    1 1/2 tsps yeast
    1 Tbs salt
    720 g flour (6 C)

Prepare the poolish the night before – dissolve the yeast in the water, stir in the flour, cover with plastic, and let it be.

The next day, toast the sunflower seeds in a 350° oven (in the middle or just above) for 12 – 16 minutes, stirring once or twice, until richly browned, but not burnt. Let these cool somewhat before proceeding.

Mix the malt syrup into the warm water in the bowl of a stand mixer (or a large mixing bowl, if working by hand). Sprinkle in the yeast, let sit a minute, then stir briefly. Add about 2/3 of the flour, then the salt, and mix with the paddle attachment (by hand this step can be done with a good wooden spoon; add the flour more gradually). Add the poolish, switch to the dough hook, and mix until the poolish is fairly well incorporated into the dough (this will take a little while – the poolish is not eager to be assimilated…). Add the sunflower seeds and continue mixing with the dough hook. The sunflower seeds, like the poolish, will resist mixing into the dough; have patience, entropy will prevail. Mix in most of the remaining flour (reserve a tablespoon or two), process, then use the reserved bit of flour to finish kneading by hand.

Transfer the dough to a large bowl, cover with plastic, and let rise 1 1/2 hours. Fold, then let rise another 1 1/2 hours.

Divide the dough in two, shape into loaves, and place in greased loaf pans. Cover these with plastic, and let rise another hour.

Preheat the oven to 400°, without convection, with a rack just below the middle. Bake for 30 minutes.

Fruit, Nut, and Seed Bread

Amazing. I know I've called some other breads the "best," but this is the best.

Yield: 3 loaves.

> 4 C warm water (946 g)
> 2 1/4 tsps yeast
> 4 tsps salt
> 3 C bread flour (360 g)
> 7 1/2 C all purpose flour (900 g)
> 1 1/2 C walnuts (180 g), coarsely chopped
> 3/4 C raw pumpkin seeds (120 g)
> 1/2 C raw sunflower seeds (75 g)
> 3/4 C dried cranberries (110 g)
> 3/4 C golden raisins (105 g)
> 3/4 C dried apricots (127 g), coarsely chopped

Mix the fruit, nuts, and seeds together.

Dissolve the yeast in the water in the bowl of a stand mixer, add the bread flour, then the salt, then about two thirds of the all purpose flour, and mix with the paddle (mixing) attachment. Add the fruit, nut, and seed mixture along with most of the remaining flour (reserve about 1/4 cup), and process with the dough hook until well kneaded. Finish kneading by hand, using the remaining flour; you can add another tablespoon or two if necessary to keep it from sticking. Cover with plastic wrap in a large bowl, and let rise for three hours, folding after an hour and a half.

Divide into three, shape into loaves, and place into greased loaf pans. Let rise one hour in the pans. Twenty minutes before the loaves are ready, preheat the oven to 400°, without convection, with a rack just below the middle. Slit the tops, then bake for 35 – 40 minutes, swapping the two outer loaves after 20 minutes to ensure even browning.

Notes:

> If you keep the walnuts in the freezer – as you certainly should – take them out as soon as you think of it, preferably the night before.

> As with almost any bread, you can of course mix and knead it by hand, instead of with a stand mixer. If you do, knead in the goodies a handful or two at a time, just before the dough gets too stiff to easily accept them.

Oat Bread

This recipe is a recently resurrected precursor to my "Best Sandwich Bread" (page 129). It has the advantage of not requiring the boiling water that the "BSB" does, and so can be made a few hours more quickly. And it's *delicious*.

Yield: 3 loaves.

>887 g warm water (3 3/4 C)
>2 1/4 tsps yeast
>1 1/2 C rolled oats
>3 Tbs molasses
>3 3/4 tsps salt
>1080 g flour (9 C)
>2 1/2 Tbs butter, plus a little more for greasing pans

Sprinkle the yeast over the water in the bowl of a stand mixer (or a large mixing bowl, if making by hand), then add the oats and molasses. Add about 2/3 of the flour, then the salt, and mix with the paddle (mixing) attachment. Add most of the remaining flour (reserve a tablespoon or two), switch to the dough hook, and process for a few minutes. Spread the remaining bit of flour on a counter to finish kneading the dough by hand, then transfer to a large bowl, cover with plastic wrap, and let rise for 3 hours, folding halfway through.

Divide the risen dough into thirds, form into loaves, and place into buttered loaf pans. Let rise one hour.

About 20 minutes before the breads are ready, preheat the oven to 400°, without convection, with a rack in the middle or just below.

Just before baking, melt the butter, slit the tops of the loaves, and brush with the butter. Bake for 30 minutes, swapping the positions of the two outer loaves after 20 minutes to promote even browning. Remove from pans immediately, and cool on racks.

Potato Bread

Soft, *pillowy*, delicious. The "recipe" is necessarily vague, as it starts with leftover mashed potatoes, and these are not all created equal.

Yield: 1 large loaf.

    1 1/2 – 2 C leftover mashed potatoes
        (seasoned – just like you had them for dinner; cold from the fridge)
    2 C hot water
    1 tsp yeast
    2 tsps salt
    about 5 – 6 C flour
    semolina (for dusting a pizza peel)

Add the hot water to the cold potatoes, along with a cup of flour (to thicken it into a more mixable consistency), and mix. The idea is for the result to be the perfect warm temperature for the yeast; if it's too hot, let it sit a while (if it's too cold I suppose you could give it a quick turn in the microwave). Once the mixture is admirably temperate, sprinkle on the yeast, and mix it in. Add the salt, and then begin adding flour, a cup at a time, until it becomes dough-like and resists stirring. Turn the dough onto a floured surface, and knead, continuing to add flour as necessary. *The dough will be sticky* – there's no way around that, so don't try to "fix" it by adding more and more flour… When it holds together and seems more or less like a bread dough, call it done. Put it in a bowl, cover with plastic wrap, and let rise for about 3 hours.

Dust a dishtowel liberally with flour, punch down the dough, form it into a ball, and then place it on the floured towel. Gather the towel up by the edges, and transfer the dough into a round mixing bowl (choose a tall one over a wide one – the goal is to keep the dough as ball-shaped as possible). Cover with plastic wrap, and let rise for 1 hour while simultaneously preheating the oven to 450°(without convection) with a baking stone on a shelf just below the middle, and a shallow pan on the floor of the oven.

Sprinkle a pizza peel with semolina. Turn the dough onto the pizza peel (so the floured side is now the top). Steam the oven by (carefully!) pouring 1/2 cup of boiling water into the pan on the oven floor – a light frying pan works best for this maneuver, and be careful not to drip on the oven window, as it is possible to crack the glass… Slide the dough onto the stone, and reduce the oven temperature to 400°. Steam the oven one more time after the bread has been baking for 10 minutes, and then continue baking for another half hour (so 40 minutes total). Remove and let cool on a wire rack.

Pita Bread

Complete with magical pocket.

Yield: 12 6-inch pitas.

> 532 g warm water (2 1/4 C)
> 1 1/2 tsps yeast
> 1 1/2 Tbs olive oil
> 1 1/4 tsps salt
> 800 g flour (6 2/3 C)

Dissolve the yeast in the water, mix in the olive oil, then add about 2/3 of the flour, then the salt, and mix. If using a stand mixer, switch to the dough hook and add the rest of the flour (reserving a tablespoon or two to finish kneading by hand). Otherwise, finish by kneading with the remainder of the flour. Transfer to a large bowl, cover with plastic, and let rise 2 hours.

Divide the dough into 12 equal pieces (accurately, by weight – the usual arithmetic is required), form into balls (with a few quick kneading folds and a little pinching up of the sides – they need not be perfect), and let rest for 20 minutes on a lightly floured surface, covered with a dish towel (plastic wrap sticks). (If you are more relaxed about the accuracy of the division, then you will also have to get a feel for the right thickness, instead of following the size guidelines below, which are tried and true…).

Preheat the oven to 475°, without convection, with a baking stone on a rack just above the middle of the oven (see notes, below).

On a floured surface, roll each ball into a circle about 6 inches in diameter – between 1/8 and 1/4 of an inch thick. These can be placed side by side on a dish towel, and then stacked with dish towels between them until all 12 are complete. Deftly invert the stack, so that when it comes time to bake them, you are starting with the first ones rolled (a pizza peel helps; you can do it). Let rest another 20 minutes.

Load the first 2 pitas on a lightly floured pizza peel, slide onto the baking stone, and bake for about 3 minutes – until the breads puff up like balloons (mine take 2 1/2 minutes, very consistently). Remove these from the oven and wrap in a dishtowel while baking the remaining breads (be careful not to get burned by steam as the breads collapse).

Notes:

Work the dough evenly when rolling it out, trying not to end up with any compressed spots that might not puff up easily. Similarly, try not to compress or stretch the dough more than necessary when transferring it from the counter to the towel where it will rest before baking.

The rest of the world bakes their pita on a very low shelf. This may help encourage them to puff up, but tends to result in an uneven pocket – in particular, the tops are often much thinner than the bottoms. I find that baking them higher in the oven alleviates this problem somewhat (and – with a little care, as described in the note above – they still puff up reliably), but quite frankly they are still not as even as I'd like. Oh well, they hold food perfectly well, and are absolutely the most delicious pita you've ever tasted – rest assured, you won't get any complaints. In any case, I confess that I am still working on perfecting these; if you figure it out before I do, let me know…

Flour Tortillas

What a revelation, that you can make your own flour tortillas. And it's easy. And they're great.

Yield: 12 small or 8 large tortillas.

> 2 C flour
> 1 tsp baking powder
> 1/2 tsp salt
> 3/4 C hot water
> 3 Tbs olive oil

Mix together the dry ingredients, the wet ingredients, and then combine them. Knead briefly on a lightly floured surface until the dough is smooth. Divide into 8 or 12 even pieces, and form these roughly into balls.

Heat a cast iron frying pan over medium high heat (you will have to gradually lower it to something more like medium as you go).

Lightly flour you work surface, and roll one of the dough balls until is it very thin – certainly less than 1/16 inch (if you are making 12, they should be about 7 – 7 1/2 inches in diameter; if you are making 8 they should be closer to 9 inches in diameter).

When the pan is hot, drop the tortilla onto it. It should take about a minute to develop some brown spots on the bottom; flip it with a metal spatula and give it another half minute on the other side. While you are cooking it you can be rolling out the next one, and thereby keeping the process moving. Pile them on a plate, wrapped in a towel, to keep them warm for dinner.

Crispy, Cheesy Breadsticks

Yum.

Yield: About 20 14-inch breadsticks.

>   237 g warm water (1 C)
>   1 1/2 tsps yeast
>   1 tsp sugar
>   1/4 C olive oil
>   1 tsp salt
>   1/2 tsp black pepper
>   3 – 4 oz finely shredded cheese
>   (such as extra sharp cheddar, aged asiago, pecorino romano, or aged gruyere)
>   390 g flour (3 1/4 C)

Sprinkle the yeast over the water, add the sugar, and stir briefly. Mix in about half the flour, then the olive oil, salt, pepper, and shredded cheese. Mix and then knead in the remaining flour. Place in a lightly oiled bowl, cover with plastic, and let rise for about 1 1/2 hours.

Preheat the oven to 400°, without convection, with a rack just above the middle. Lightly oil two half sheet pans.

Roll the dough out about 1/4 inch thick on an unfloured surface. Cut into 1/2 inch strips (a pizza cutting wheel works well for this). Lift each strip, give it a number of twists, and let it stretch just a little – not too much – as you carry it over to the baking tray. Depending on the shape of your rolled dough, it will probably work best to lay the strips the long way across the tray (if any are too long, cut them in half). Leave a little space between them so they can expand a bit without touching. Once you've filled a tray (with about half the breadsticks), bake for 17 – 18 minutes, until browned somewhat but not burned, while you work on the next tray. Let cool a minute or two before removing to racks to cool completely.

Notes:

>   It may be necessary to rotate the tray partway through the baking to encourage even browning.
>
>   Places where the breadsticks get too thin during the stretching and twisting are likely to burn…

Breadcrumbs

If you've taken my advice to slice and freeze your breads the day you make them, then eventually bags of mystery bread that no one will eat, whose origins are entirely forgotten, will begin to accumulate in the freezer. From these we make breadcrumbs…

(The rest of the world makes breadcrumbs from stale bread, which is all well and good, but I never have any. So these are a little different – technically they are "toasted" breadcrumbs; you can use them the same way you'd use any other breadcrumbs.)

    Sliced bread

    Optional: basil, oregano, garlic powder, and grated pecorino romano cheese

Lay out the bread slices on cookie sheets and bake them in a low oven, turning them over now and then, until they're thoroughly dried – they should snap in half when you break them, and not bend at all. 300° or so is about right; I usually have two shelves going and switch the trays from one to the other when I turn the slices over. Convection probably helps speed the drying process. Thicker slices take longer; you can remove the slices as they're done, and leave only the ones that need more time. If you run out of patience, fine – call it good enough, but pass the end results through a wire strainer to remove the oversized bits – any slices that are still pliable won't crumble finely.

When the bread is dry, run it through a food processor. To make "seasoned" breadcrumbs, mix in the optional ingredients, to taste. (Unless otherwise specified, my recipes that include breadcrumbs assume that they are seasoned.)

Pizza

General Notes

First of all, you absolutely *need* a baking stone or steel, and to make the 13 – 14 inch pizzas I describe, it will have to be at least 14 inches in its smallest dimension. Mine are 14 × 16 inches, which works well. I suppose if you must settle for something smaller, then you can adjust the recipes accordingly. You also absolutely need a pizza peel, and if you are ever going to make more than one pizza – which *of course* you are – then you really need two – that way you can prepare the second pizza on one peel while keeping the other free to remove the first pizza from the oven. This is actually not bad news at all, as it is helpful to have one wooden peel and one metal peel; the wooden peel is preferable for getting the pizza into the oven, and the metal peel for getting it out. Make sure that the peels you buy match the size of your stone or steel, and in particular, they should be roughly 14 inches in both dimensions. You have no need for an especially long handle – those are for professionals with deep pizza ovens.

If you choose to get a baking steel, 1/4 inch is a reasonable thickness. It will be surprisingly heavy. Half inch is really going overboard, and 1/8 inch is probably too thin to retain the heat properly.

Okay, we will assume that you have made the dough according to the instructions on page 151, and gathered up and prepared whatever other ingredients you need for the recipe(s) you intend to make. About 45 minutes before you're ready to start making pizzas (so about an hour before you want the first one to come out of the oven), preheat the oven to 550°, with convection, with your baking stone or steel on a rack in the upper part of the oven (about 8 inches or so from the top).

Note: I use convection here because my oven seems to keep a more consistent temperature when I do, and seeing as the pizza will only bake for a few minutes, it's important that the oven stays hot. Do what works best with your oven. Hotter is definitely better, but honestly I am afraid to go higher than 550° (and my 550° with convection is 525° without – see page 3) – the modern oven is a very hot box with a computer on top of it, and computers and heat are a notoriously bad combination. (You say "but it's designed for this situation." Yes. But most people never turn it up past 450°, and the company that designed it will shed no tears if you have to replace the motherboard now and then. Which is to say that if you can set your oven to 600° or higher – which I'm not at all sure you can – you might make better pizza, but you might also go through ovens almost as fast as you go through pizzas. Try it, what do I know. But try it long before your warranty period expires…)

Moving right along. Pizza dough is *stretched*, not rolled, and everybody does it differently. If you want my advice, *don't try to learn it from me* – go find two or three different videos on how to stretch a pizza dough, and see how the professionals do it. Or walk into your local pizza place, order a pizza, and *watch*. Ask questions, if you're feeling bold.

But okay, here we are, a bunch of pizza recipes follow, and I feel some moral obligation to try to explain how to stretch a pizza dough. So I will give it a shot.

Uncover your fully risen dough ball, dust the top with flour, and ease it out onto a well floured surface. Pat some flour up around the edges, so that the entire dough is well dusted. Press the dough ball into a round disk with your hands, then go around the edge with your fingertips making indentations for the edge of the crust, about half an inch in from the edges – in other words, you are using your fingertips to press in and delineate where the flat, thin "body" of the pizza ends, and the puffy "crust" of the pizza – the part you pick it up by – begins.

The goal now is to stretch the part in the middle until it is uniformly thin, while leaving the edges a little puffy, and manipulating the whole thing to have a diameter of 13 – 14 inches. Almost all of this is done on the floured surface (keep adding flour as necessary to keep the dough from sticking); when it is nearly done you will complete the final shaping and stretching on the (preferably wooden) pizza peel.

How to do this? The fanciest, trained professional method, includes laying the dough across the backs of your hands and wrists, gently stretching it, turning it, and even – very impressively – tossing it up into the air for a spin. Try it, if you like. I can make some progress along these lines, and the toss is not even the part that gives me significant trouble (it's easier than it looks), but I invariably end up with a dough that stretches too thinly in the middle – I have not yet succeeded in getting the parts closer to edge to thin consistently. But practice makes perfect, and if you want to go this route, by all means, have at it.

Here is a more conservative approach. Put your hands side by side, and lay your fingertips into the indentation you made along the edge on one side of the dough. Press down lightly with your fingers and the upper parts of your hands, and gently spread the dough apart, keeping the edge mostly intact. Rotate the dough, and repeat with the adjacent section. Work your way around the dough in this manner, stretching it as evenly as possible. Stop and check every now and then for thicker sections, and stretch them thinner. You can also grasp the puffed up edge of the dough between the thumbs and forefingers of both hands, and lift and stretch the dough this way – this technique works well in conjunction with the pressing and stretching technique just described. If you need to pull in a little dough that you "reserved" for the edge to get the middle stretched to size, that's okay, too. And if you happen to stretch the dough too much and end up with a hole someplace, just pinch together some of the surrounding dough and patch it up.

When the dough is nearly the size and shape you want, *very* lightly dust a pizza peel with flour – sprinkle some on, and then mostly wipe it off. It helps if the pizza peel is wood (the moist dough is more apt to stick to a metal peel), and if you are nervous about it, or the first few times you try it, you can use semolina instead of flour – the pizza slides off the semolina more easily (but then you have a pizza with semolina on the bottom, instead of a barely discernible dusting of flour). Slide one arm entirely under one side of the dough, grasp the other side with your other hand, and lift the dough onto the pizza peel. It will stretch and deform, and hang off the peel in places – don't worry, that's all okay. Just gather it up, reform it into a nice circle, check that it is as large as you want it, and if not, give it a little extra stretching, right on the peel.

Once the dough is ready, it's best not to dally. Not that you have to rush, but the longer the dough sits on the peel, the more likely it is to absorb the flour underneath it, and stick. In other words, don't transfer the dough to the peel until you're ready to make the pizza.

Okay, your dough is on the peel, your oven is ready. Top the pizza however you intend. Lift the peel by the handle and give it a *slight* forward and backward jerk – your intention is to ensure that the pizza is not stuck to the peel, or to loosen it if it is just slightly stuck, *before* you are trying to slide it onto a hot stone or steel in a hot oven. Then open the oven and deftly and gracefully slide the pizza off the peel and onto the stone or steel – it's the same forward and backward jerk you practiced a moment ago, but with the backward part greatly emphasized. I like to let the front tip of the peel touch the stone (or steel) near the back of the oven at the beginning of this maneuver.

It sounds complicated and difficult. Really, it just takes some practice. Expect to screw it up a few times – the results will be messy and disfigured, and delicious anyway. I have had lots of practice, and it almost always goes well, but occasionally I still stick a pizza to the back wall of the oven, drape it over the front edge of the stone, or roll the toppings off in every direction. Some swearing ensues, maybe a little smoke. Nobody goes hungry.

Pizza cooks quickly, so keep an eye on it – especially if it is the last one, and you felt entitled to sit down and eat a slice of a previous pizza with your family or guests. ("Don't let me forget the one that's in the oven" you'll say. Nobody will help; it is all on you.) When it is ready, slide a peel under it – a metal peel works better here, but a wooden one will do – and remove it to a cutting board. If you can give it a minute to let the cheese set just a little before slicing, it will come out prettier, but in any event, slice and serve. Don't burn your mouth – the pizza is *hot*.

Note: Probably the procedure above will yield superb results, but if you find that the bottom of the crust doesn't develop some nice dark mottling, you can set the oven to broil for a minute or two before you are ready to load the pizza into the oven. Immediately turn the oven back down to 550° (with convection) once you've put the pizza in.

If you are using a baking stone and not steel, then this might be a bad idea – baking stones can withstand very hot temperatures, but they are not made to withstand rapid temperature *changes*. Try it, if you like – it will probably be fine. But maybe not. This is really the only capacity in which a pizza steel may be preferable to stone (and the chances are you will not need to do this anyway).

Pizza Dough

This recipe is designed for a pizza with a thin bottom crust but a generous edge crust, and a diameter of at least 13 inches and preferably closer to 14 inches – pretty much the limit of what will fit on a standard pizza stone or steel. Scale it as needed if you make your pizzas differently.

You can make a *great* pizza dough with all purpose flour, but if you want to go all out, bread flour will make a *slightly* better one. Since the amount of protein (hence gluten) differs, the quantities are not exactly the same.

For convenience, the following table gives the quantities of water, salt, and flour (or bread flour) for up to five pizzas (you also need yeast, which we will consider next):

	1 pizza	2 pizzas	3 pizzas	4 pizzas	5 pizzas
water:	193 g	386 g	579 g	772 g	965 g
salt:	7 g	14 g	21 g	28 g	35 g
flour:	275 g	550 g	825 g	1100 g	1375 g
	– or –	– or –	– or –	– or –	– or –
bread flour:	265 g	530 g	795 g	1060 g	1325 g

The amount of yeast to use depends on how much time you have before baking the pizza, as well as the temperature of your water (which should be warm) and of your house (which should also be warm…). Use these amounts as a rough guide; adjust them as experience dictates:

> 2 hours: 1.5 g yeast per pizza (about 1/2 tsp).
> 3 hours: 1.2 g yeast per pizza (about 2/5 tsp).
> 4 – 6 hours: 0.7 g yeast per pizza (about 1/4 tsp).
> 9 – 10 hours: 0.4 g yeast per pizza (about 1/8 tsp).

Yes, you can still make pizza, even if you only have two hours for the dough to rise. In theory the dough will be tastier if it rises longer, but in practice, it will be delicious regardless. Perhaps if you tasted them side by side you'd be able to tell the difference, but since that will never happen (when are you going to make pizza dough twice, hours apart, for the same meal?), you may as well call it just as good.

Directions:

Stir the salt into the water until fully dissolved, then sprinkle in the yeast and allow to sit until it sinks – about a minute – before stirring. Add the flour, mix briefly with a spoon, then continue mixing, pinching, squeezing, and kneading with your hands for about a minute, until the dough is reasonably uniform. (Medical gloves are a big help here, otherwise you'll be picking dough out of the hairs on your hands for the rest of the day.) Cover and let rest for 20 minutes.

Turn the dough out onto a lightly floured surface and knead very briefly – just a few, quick strokes (you are only partially kneading the dough here; you will finish momentarily), then divide it into equal portions (one per pizza). Finish kneading each portion (also briefly – maybe half a minute), and shape them into tight balls by folding and stretching; stop before the dough starts to tear. Let rise in lightly oiled, covered containers until ready to make pizzas.

The dough can also be refrigerated overnight; use 1 g yeast per pizza, and after dividing the dough into separate containers let it rise for two hours before refrigerating. Remove the dough from the refrigerator an hour or so before making the pizzas.

Note: It just so happens that each pizza dough will weigh pretty darn close to 1 pound, in case you happen to need a 1 pound pizza dough for something.

Pizza Sauce
Adapted from "The Elements of Pizza" by Ken Forkish.

Canned tomatoes are not all created equal – far from it – and what you use will have a profound effect on your sauce. Ideally you will find good quality whole tomatoes packed in tomato puree, preferably with no added salt, and no basil. The salt is negotiable – if your can has more than 30 mg sodium per 1/2 cup serving, decrease the salt in the recipe accordingly. And the basil is not a plus, but you can probably fish most of it out and discard it. But if it's packed in juice, the sauce you make will be thin and watery. And if the tomatoes themselves are lacking in flavor, you can't expect better for the sauce.

After my supermarket stopped carrying the only brand I was satisfied with (*Boticelli*), I started using *Pomi* brand "strained" tomatoes. This is a seedless puree with no ingredients other than tomatoes. It comes in a 700 gram box, so I decrease the other ingredients slightly (28 ounces is just shy of 800 grams, so 7 grams of salt and 14 grams of sugar is just about right). Also, since the tomatoes are already pureed, it is possible to take the lazy way out and skip the blender – replace the garlic with a little garlic powder, and don't worry that the crushed red pepper doesn't get blended. It's not quite as good, but it's close, and there's less cleanup.

- 1 28 oz can whole peeled tomatoes
- 1 1/2 Tbs olive oil
- 1 clove garlic, crushed
- 8 g salt
- 0.3 g oregano (about 1/2 tsp)
- 0.4 g crushed red pepper (about 1/8 tsp)
- 15 g sugar (1 Tbs)

Put the olive oil, garlic, salt, oregano, red pepper, and sugar in a blender, and add a few spoonfuls of the liquid that the tomatoes are packed in. Blend well, scraping down the sides with a rubber spatula once or twice. Add the remainder of the tomatoes, and give it a few quick pulses, until the tomatoes are broken down into a coarse sauce – no big pieces, but also not perfectly smooth.

Transfer the sauce to a deep saucepan, and bring to a vigorous simmer over medium heat. Continue to simmer for 10 or 15 minutes, then set aside to cool.

New York Style Pizza

This is as close to the pizza I grew up loving as I have been able to come. I think that to do better you'd need an oven that could reach 700° or so. Enjoy.

    135 g pizza sauce (page 153)
    15 g pecorino romano cheese, finely grated
    132 g mozzarella, coarsely grated

    1 pizza dough (page 151)

Follow the "general directions" (page 148).

To form the pizza, first spread the sauce, then the romano cheese, and finally the mozzarella.

Take the pizza out when it begins to get some dark spots; it won't take long (about 5 minutes), so keep an eye on it. Let cool for a minute or two before slicing.

Vegetarian Sausage
Adapted from "Seitan and Beyond" by Skye Michael Conroy.

The fact is that a plain, New York style pizza really can't be beat. Nevertheless, the "spice of life" being what it is, there are times when a variation is in order. For those times, there's this – a fine, spicy, vegetarian sausage that you can cut up and use as a pizza topping.

These require overnight refrigeration to develop the proper texture, so start them a day (or more) before you want them at the dinner table.

1 C vital wheat gluten
1 Tbs garbanzo bean (chickpea) flour
1 Tbs dried minced onion
2 tsps onion powder
2 tsps whole fennel seeds, divided
1 1/4 C water
2 Tbs soy sauce
1 Tbs olive oil
2 tsps crushed red pepper
1 tsp oregano
1 tsp basil
1/2 tsp ground black or white pepper
1/4 tsp salt

Optional: 1 tsp liquid smoke

Mix the vital wheat gluten, garbanzo bean flour, dried minced onion, onion powder, and 1 teaspoon of the fennel seeds in a medium mixing bowl. Combine all of the remaining ingredients in a blender, and blend until smooth. Add the wet ingredients to the dry, and mix for a minute or two with a silicone spatula (or, if you don't have one, a wooden spoon) – not just to combine, but also to develop the gluten. Let rest five minutes.

Divide into 4 – 6 more or less equal parts (depending on how big you want the sausages), and roll each one tightly in a square of aluminum foil (preferably "heavy duty" aluminum foil) to form sausage shapes. Carefully twist the ends of the foil to seal. If you tear the foil at all, roll it in a second piece of foil outside the first.

Bring two or three inches of water to a rolling boil in the base of a large steamer. Add the foil packets, and steam for 45 minutes. Remove the sausages from the steamer, let cool to room temperature (if you have the time and patience – if not, do what you can), and refrigerate – still wrapped in foil – overnight.

When you're ready to use these, remove them from the foil, and brown them in a frying pan with a little oil over medium heat before slicing for a pizza topping.

Sicilian Pizza
Adapted from "The Elements of Pizza" by Ken Forkish

Start making the dough about 5 3/4 hours before you want to eat.

Serves 4.

Dough:

> 375 g warm water
> 11 g salt
> 2 g yeast
> 500 g flour

Topping:

> 350 g pizza sauce (page 153), divided
> 200 g mozzarella
> 30 g pecorino romano cheese
> 4 Tbs olive oil, divided

Dissolve the salt in the water; sprinkle on the yeast. Let rest a minute, stir, then stir in the flour. Mix by hand (with medical gloves), mostly squeezing the dough between your fingers, but occasionally folding it over itself, until uniform. Cover, and let rest for 20 minutes.

Turn the dough onto a lightly floured surface, and knead briefly, until smooth. Place in a lightly oiled bowl, cover, and let rise for about 4 hours.

After the rising time, place a baking stone or steel on the very lowest shelf of the oven, and heat the oven to 525°, with convection.

Turn the dough out onto a lightly floured surface, and work it into a roughly rectangular shape. Spread 3 tablespoons of olive oil on a half sheet pan, including the sides, and transfer the dough to the pan (support half of it on your extended forearm; lift the other half with your remaining hand). Stretch the dough to more or less fit the pan, trying to keep it fairly even in thickness. Spread the remaining tablespoon of olive oil over the surface of the dough (fingers are the best tool for this…), let rest 10 minutes, then finish spreading the dough to the edges of the pan. Let rise another 30 minutes while the oven (and stone or steel) heats up.

Spread 200 grams of tomato sauce evenly on the dough, leaving 1/4 inch or so bare at the edges, and bake for 10 – 12 minutes (with the pan resting on the stone or steel), until dark spots begin to appear on the sauce. Remove from the oven, spread the remaining 150 grams of sauce on the pizza, then sprinkle with the romano cheese, and finally top with the mozzarella. Return the pizza to the oven, and bake until the cheese develops some dark spots.

Slide the pizza out of the pan and onto a wooden cutting board as soon as it comes out of the oven. Let cool for about two minutes before slicing.

"Dancing Heart" Pizza

Inspired by the pizza of the same name that they make at *American Flatbread* in Burlington, Vermont. I have no idea where the name comes from, but I like it.

    5 oz aged asiago
    thinly sliced garlic
    sesame seeds
    olive oil

    1 pizza dough (page 151)

Brush the crust with olive oil, then spread the cheese, and top with sliced garlic and a generous sprinkling of sesame seeds. Bake as described in the "general directions" (page 148).

Note: Use well-aged asiago – it should have a noticeably dark color – or else try *American Grana*.

Macaroni and Cheese Pizza

Tell yourself that you're making it for the kids, if you like, but count on the adults eating more than their share… Really good stuff.

    5 oz elbow pasta
    1 1/3 C milk
    2 Tbs flour
    2 Tbs oil
    1/2 tsp salt
    3/4 tsp onion powder
    4.5 oz extra sharp cheddar

    1 pizza dough (page 151)

Cook the pasta until al dente, rinse thoroughly under cold water (to stop it from cooking any further), and set aside.

Scald the milk over medium heat in a small, heavy bottomed saucepan, stirring occasionally (it need not boil). When the milk is nearly ready, make the roux: Combine the flour, oil, onion powder, and salt in a saucepan and cook over medium-low heat until it starts to bubble. Turn the heat down to very low and whisk in the milk a little at a time, until it is all added. Add the cheese and stir until it is melted (just a minute or two), and mix the sauce into the pasta.

Spread evenly over the pizza dough, and bake according to the "general directions" (page 148).

Potato Pizza

This is my most popular pizza. Delicious. Amazing.

>   2 small russet potatoes
>   1/2 small onion, sliced
>   2 oz aged asiago
>   2 oz sharp cheddar
>   2 oz aged gruyere
>   2 oz mozzarella
>   a few sprigs of parsley
>   vegetable oil, for frying
>
>   1 pizza dough (page 151)

Peel the potatoes and slice them into thin rounds, between 1/16 and 1/8 of an inch thick. Arrange these on microwavable plates, with as little contact as possible between slices – they will glue themselves to each other where they touch. Microwave on high for about 4 or 5 minutes, until partially cooked. (They will glue themselves down somewhat and need to be teased gently from the plates – you can do it.)

Coat the bottom of a wide frying pan with about 1/4 inch of oil, and set the pan over a high heat. When the oil is hot, fry the potatoes in batches, without crowding the pan, turning the potatoes over once or twice, until they are browned and crisp. Drain each batch briefly on paper towels before removing to wire racks to cool.

Grate the cheeses and mix them together.

To assemble the pizza, sprinkle 2/3 of the cheese over the dough, then arrange the potato slices, and top with the remaining cheese and then the onion slices. Bake according to the "general directions" (page 148).

A minute or two before the pizza is done, remove it from the oven and scatter the parsley over the top, then return it to the oven to finish baking.

Notes:

>   Asiago that isn't aged is a whole different beast, and I don't recommend it. If you can't find aged asiago, try *American Grana*, which is similar, or else a well-aged parmesan.
>
>   Similarly, gruyere that isn't suitably aged is disappointing. You can probably find good, aged gruyere, but you might have to overcome your shock at how expensive it is. Go for it anyway – you get what you pay for.

You can also substitute smoked gruyere for a nice variation.

Microwaves vary – if the potatoes don't turn out reasonably crispy, increase the amount of time in the microwave.

Old Bay Pizza

Seared shrimp in *Old Bay* seasoning on pizza; what could be better?

The reasoning behind the two types of *Old Bay* is to get the most flavor possible without making the pizza overly salty.

    1 lb 26-30 shrimp
    2 oz mozzarella
    1.5 oz sharp provolone
    1.5 oz aged asiago
    2 tsps *low sodium* Old Bay seasoning
    1 tsp (regular) Old Bay seasoning
    oil

    1 pizza dough (page 151)

Heat a little oil in a wide, heavy bottomed pot until very hot, then add the shrimp in a single layer. Sear for a minute or two without stirring, then turn over each shrimp and sear the other side. Remove from the heat when they are nearly cooked through; they will finish cooking on the pizza in the oven.

Top the pizza with the mixed grated cheeses, then the shrimp, then sprinkle the Old Bay seasoning all over. Bake according to the "general directions" (page 148).

Scallion Pancake Pizza

All the scallion pancake goodness, but baked instead of fried, and bigger as well. Amazing.

Pizza:

    1 bunch scallions (green parts only)
    3 – 4 Tbs toasted sesame oil
    1 tsp sesame seeds (optional)

    1 pizza dough (page 151)

Dipping Sauce:

    2 Tbs soy sauce
    2 Tbs water
    1 Tbs rice vinegar
    3/4 tsp toasted sesame oil
    1 1/4 tsps sugar
    1 tsp fresh ginger, minced
    1 small scallion, green part only, minced
    1/4 tsp crushed red pepper flakes (optional)

Make the dipping sauce first (mix together all the ingredients) – it benefits from sitting for a while.

For the pizza, roll the dough out thinly (into a circle with a diameter of about 17 or 18 inches). Brush it generously with sesame oil (not quite to the edge), then scatter the scallions all over it. Roll it up tightly into a long log shape, seal the ends and the seam (as best you can without working too hard), then form it into a spiral shape, tucking the outside end under a bit to finish.

Press the spiral flat with your hands, then roll it into a 13 inch diameter circle. (It will fight back; do your best. If you have the time to let it rest a few minutes, that will help, but if not, just force it. In the end it will win – even after you get it large enough, it will shrink back some.) Transfer to a floured pizza peel, brush with more sesame oil, sprinkle with sesame seeds (if you like), and bake it according to the "general directions" (page 148).

Note: Making true scallion pancakes is not all that different: Instead of pizza dough, pour 1 cup of boiling water into 3 cups of flour, mix, and knead until smooth. Cover with a damp cloth for an hour, then form into a 4 inch cylinder and cut into 4 1-inch disks with a sharp knife. Roll these out and form them into pancakes as described above, dividing the scallions among the pancakes (maybe sprinkling with a pinch of salt, and certainly omitting the sesame seeds). Fry each one in a mixture of toasted sesame and vegetable oils. Very delicious, but also greasy…

Grilled Pizza
Inspired by grill master Bill Kane, who first showed me it could be done.

Pizza on the grill – *so cool*. Individual-sized pizzas are easier to handle, and afford the opportunity for everyone to assemble their own, choosing what they like for toppings. Personally, my favorite is sliced pears, gorgonzola, walnuts, and a light drizzle of honey. I recommend avoiding wet foods like fresh mozzarella and sliced tomatoes; the pizzas cook quickly on the grill, so they don't dry much, and you end up with a bit of a drippy mess. But experiment, use your imagination, and have fun.

I use the same ratio of flour to water as I do in my standard pizza dough (page 151), but a little less salt, and about half the yeast. With those modifications, one standard pizza dough makes about three individual grilled pizzas, and you can start from that recipe and scale up or down based on how many pizza eaters you have, or else use the recipe below, scaled for four.

Yield: 4 individual-sized grilled pizzas.

>   233 g water
>   7 g salt
>   0.4 g yeast (about 1/8 tsp)
>   333 g flour
>
>   olive oil
>   toppings…

As with a standard pizza dough, mix the salt into the water, sprinkle on the yeast, let it sit a minute, then stir to dissolve. Mix in the flour, first with a spoon, and then with your hands (preferably protected by medical gloves; use the squeezing-through-your-fingers technique described in the standard pizza dough recipe). Let sit, covered, for 20 minutes, then knead briefly, divide into 4 equal pieces, and form into balls. Spread a generous amount of olive oil around an 8 × 12 × 2 inch baking tray, roll the balls around a bit so they get coated, and then place them as far apart from each other as you can. Cover with plastic wrap, and let rise for about 6 hours. (For more than 4 pizzas, use a larger tray…)

To grill the pizzas: Start the grill and bring it up to a medium heat. Spread plenty of olive oil on a work surface, and transfer a dough ball to the surface. Flip the dough to coat both sides with oil, then flatten it out some with your hands. Finish with a rolling pin, keeping the dough (and the rolling pin) well oiled, and rolling it out until it is roughly 1/8 of an inch thick – about 10 inches in diameter. Assuming your grill can fit two such pizzas at a time, do the same with a second dough ball. Brush the grill with olive oil, then transfer the dough to the grill (just use your hands – pick it up and flop it on there…– it will distort some, which is fine). When the bottom sides are cooked (which only takes a few minutes), remove the partially cooked pizza doughs from the grill and flip them over, so that your pizza eaters can arrange their desired toppings on the cooked side of the dough. Do the same for the next pair of dough balls.

When the topped pizzas are ready, brush the grill again with olive oil, and transfer the pizzas to the grill. Close the lid to encourage the cheese to melt, and remove the pizzas when the bottoms are done cooking.

Notes:

If the dough cooks before the cheese melts, you can try grilling over a lower heat, or if your grill has a warming rack, try using that for a little while.

You can of course let your pizza doughs rise for more time or less; adjust the yeast accordingly (see the guidelines on page 151; remember to use about half the amount suggested there).

Focaccia

Start about 3 1/2 hours before dinner (that includes letting the dough cool for 15 minutes or so before serving).

Dough:

    473 g warm water (2 C)
    2 tsps yeast
    3/8 C olive oil
    2 tsps salt
    750 g flour (6 1/4 C)

Toppings:

    olive oil
    sliced onion
    sliced garlic
    dried basil
    dried oregano
    flaked sea salt

In the bowl of a stand mixer, dissolve the yeast in the water (you can also do this by hand, of course, but I will continue to assume you are using a stand mixer). Add about 4 cups of the flour, the olive oil, and the salt, and mix with the paddle attachment. Switch to the dough hook, add almost all of the remaining flour (reserve about a tablespoon for final kneading), and knead well. Finish kneading, briefly, by hand, cover with plastic wrap, and let rise about an hour and a half.

Spread 2 or 3 tablespoons of olive oil in a half sheet pan or large cookie sheet. Flatten the dough into a rough rectangle, then transfer to the pan and shape to fit, working your fingertips into the dough to dimple it all over. Brush generously with olive oil, add toppings, and press these into the dough. Let rise about an hour before baking.

Preheat the oven to 425°, with convection, with a shelf in the lower part of the oven. Bake for about 20 minutes, until nicely browned.

Focaccia with Leeks
Adapted from "Focaccia" by Carol Field

Starter:

    1/2 C warm water (118 g)
    0.5 g yeast
    160 g flour (1 1/3 C)

Dough:

    1 8 oz potato
    1 C milk (245 g)
    1/4 C warm water
    1 1/2 tsps yeast
    1 Tbs olive oil
    1 egg
    520 g flour (4 1/3 C)
    2 1/2 tsps salt

Topping:

    5 Tbs olive oil, divided
    3 large leeks
    1/4 tsp salt

You can make the starter the night before, or in the morning; most of the time I forget and make it right when I start making the focaccia, which is fine. Dissolve the yeast in the water, then mix in the flour until you have a rough dough. Set it aside until you're ready to start.

Start about four hours before you want the focaccia to come out of the oven. Peel, thickly slice, and boil the potato until it's soft, then mash it – a potato ricer or food mill is ideal. Let the mashed potato cool enough so that it won't harm the yeast.

Warm the egg by placing it in a bowl of hot tap water, and warm the milk a little in the microwave. Combine the milk and water in the bowl of a stand mixer (or in a large mixing bowl, if mixing by hand), sprinkle in the yeast, let settle for a minute, then stir to dissolve. Add the olive oil, the egg (lightly beaten), and the mashed potato. Add the starter in small pieces, mix briefly, then add about 2/3 of the flour, followed by the salt. Mix with the paddle attachment until the dough is uniform, then add the remaining flour, switch to the dough hook, and continue mixing for a few minutes. The dough should be smooth and elastic, but still rather moist. Use an additional tablespoon or two of flour to finish up kneading the dough by hand, then transfer to a lightly oiled bowl, cover with plastic wrap, and let rise for 1 1/2 hours.

While the dough is rising, prepare the topping. Slice the leeks thinly, using just the white parts, and clean them by soaking in a bowl of cold water briefly, then lifting (not pouring) them out with a strainer or slotted spoon. Sauté the leeks in 3 tablespoons of the olive oil over very low heat in a wide frying pan for 20 minutes, stirring frequently, then cover and continue to cook over the lowest possible heat for another ten minutes, stirring once or twice. If they stick, add a little water. Try not to let them brown – they'll brown in the oven.

Oil a half sheet pan (or large cookie sheet). When the dough is ready, turn it out onto a lightly floured surface, stretch it into a rough rectangle (somewhat smaller than the pan), then lift it into the pan and coax it to fit. Drizzle the remaining 2 tablespoons of olive oil over the dough, spread it around with your fingers, and set aside to rise for another hour.

About 45 minutes before the dough is done rising, preheat the oven to 400°, without convection, with a baking stone on a rack just above the middle.

When the dough is ready, poke your fingers down into it all over, then spread the leek topping evenly over it. Sprinkle with the salt, and bake (with the pan on the baking stone) for about 25 minutes, until nicely browned.

Herbed Flatbread
Inspired by James McNair's "Vegetarian Pizza"

Yield: 4 flatbreads.

>355 g warm water (1 1/2 C)
>2 tsps yeast
>1 1/2 tsps sugar
>1 1/2 tsps salt
>6 Tbs olive oil (plus more for brushing)
>600 g flour (5 C)
>chopped fresh herbs (quantity and variety is up to you; good choices include marjoram, sage, basil, oregano, parsley, chives, scallions).
>
>coarse or flaked salt (optional)

Dissolve the yeast in the water, mix in the sugar. Add the olive oil and about 2/3 of the flour, and mix well (by hand or in a stand mixer). Mix in the salt and herbs, then either knead in the remainder of the flour, or mix it in with the dough hook (reserving a tablespoon or two to finish kneading by hand). Cover with plastic wrap, and let rise for about 2 hours.

About 45 minutes before the dough is ready, preheat the oven to 500°, without convection, with a baking stone (or steel) on a high shelf.

Divide the dough into four pieces. For each piece, roll it out to 15 or 16 inches (it will shrink to 13 or 14 inches), transfer it to a lightly floured pizza peel, brush it with olive oil, and poke holes all over it with a fork (to try to keep major bubbles from forming). Sprinkle lightly with coarse salt, if you like, and bake until nicely browned, about 5 or 6 minutes.

Notes:

>These are a nice vehicle for *Surfer Spread* (page 85).
>
>You can also cook these on the grill – divide the dough into 6 pieces, and follow the directions for *Grilled Pizza* on page 166.

Soup

Simple But Excellent Carrot Soup

The title says it all.

    2 lbs carrots, peeled and chopped
    4 C vegetable stock (page 184)
    1/3 C slivered almonds
    2 Tbs butter
    1 C chopped onion
    1 or 2 cloves garlic, crushed
    1 C water (or an additional cup of vegetable stock)
    salt
    white pepper

    Garnish: toasted almonds, croutons, parsley, chives, sautéed mushrooms, or fried shallots.

Bring the carrots to a boil in the 4 cups of stock, cover, and simmer for about 15 minutes. Remove from the heat and let cool somewhat. Sauté the almonds in the butter until they take on just a little bit of color, then add the onions, garlic, and a couple of pinches of salt, and continue cooking until the onions are soft and translucent (but not browned).

Add the cup of water (or stock), and puree everything together in a blender, working in small batches, until very smooth.

Return to the stove and heat gently. Adjust the salt as needed (the amount will depend on the salt content of the stock), and season with white pepper to taste. Serve with one of the garnishes listed above.

Note: It turns out that not all carrots are created equal; it is possible to buy nearly flavorless carrots, resulting in a correspondingly disappointing soup. Certainly anything that doesn't appear to be quite fresh is suspect, and I would also avoid carrots that are splitting or unusually large. A deep orange color is a good sign.

African Peanut Soup

Use homemade vegetable stock (page 184) and a good, natural peanut butter (with nothing other than peanuts and possibly salt). The kashmiri chili powder is certainly not authentically African, but it's delicious and goes well. If you don't have it, leave it out; maybe substitute a pinch of cayenne, if you like. And it's best if you use raw peanuts and roast them yourself (in the oven, at 350° until darkened somewhat; 15 – 20 minutes or so). You can add them directly to the soup, but if there are leftovers the peanuts will be soggy, so it's prudent to serve them as a garnish.

    4 C vegetable stock (page 184)
    1 medium onion
    1 large carrot
    1 small sweet potato (or yam – what's the difference? – don't tell me.)
    1/2 C peanut butter
    3 oz (half can) tomato paste
    0 – 1 1/2 tsp salt (depending on the broth and the peanut butter)
    1/2 tsp kashmiri chili powder
    1/2 C peanuts, roasted

Chop the onion and fry it in a little vegetable oil, then set it aside. Peel the carrot and the sweet potato, and cut the carrot into coins, and the sweet potato into small cubes (at most 1/2 inch). Add the carrots and sweet potato to the broth, bring to a boil, then lower to a simmer.

In a small mixing bowl, mix together the peanut butter, tomato paste, and chili powder. Slowly mix in hot broth, a little at a time, until the result is smooth and fluid. Mix this into the broth, and continue simmering until the sweet potatoes and carrots are soft. Adjust the salt to taste, mix in the onions, and serve garnished with the roasted peanuts.

Potato Cheese Soup
Adapted from "Laurel's Kitchen"
by Laurel Robertson, Carol Flanders, and Bronwen Godfrey.

Hearty, filling, and delicious.

    4 C thickly sliced potatoes (26 – 28 oz.)
    3 1/2 C water
    2 tsps salt, divided
    1 small onion, sliced
    1 Tbs oil
    2 C milk
    6 oz extra sharp cheddar, grated
    1/4 tsp white pepper (or black, if that's what you have)

Put the potatoes in a 4 quart saucepan, add the water and 1 1/2 teaspoons of salt, cover, bring to a boil, and cook until tender. While the potatoes are boiling, sauté the onion in the oil until soft and translucent. Thoroughly puree the potatoes with their cooking water and the sautéed onions in two or three batches in a blender.

Return the soup to the saucepan, add the milk and the pepper, and cook over low heat. When the soup is hot, add the grated cheese, and stir until melted. Taste, and adjust the salt as you see fit – the remaining 1/2 teaspoon should be just about right.

Notes:

Waxy potatoes such as red, white, or Yukon gold work better than starchy potatoes like russets, which may not blend as smoothly.

You can use vegetable stock (page 184) instead of water; decrease the salt accordingly.

Seafood Soup

A true treat for seafood lovers.

Serves 3 or 4, as a main dish.

    4 C milk
    5 Tbs flour
    1/2 tsp thyme
    1/2 tsp onion powder
    4 Tbs oil
    1 1/4 tsps salt
    1 bay leaf
    2 Tbs white wine
    black pepper
    1 medium-small potato, cut into 1/2 inch cubes
    1/2 lb bay scallops
    1/2 lb salmon, cut into 1/2 inch cubes
    1/2 lb small shrimp

Heat the milk to scalding.

In a large saucepan, make a roux from the flour, spices, and oil, and cook over medium high heat until bubbling. Turn the heat down to low, then whisk in the milk, a little at a time. Add the salt, bay leaf, wine, and a few grinds of black pepper, and bring to a simmer.

Add the potatoes to the soup and simmer for 25 minutes. Then add the scallops and simmer for another 10 minutes. Finally add the shrimp and salmon and simmer for 5 – 10 minutes more, until these last additions are thoroughly cooked.

Remove the bay leaf and serve immediately.

Vegetable Stock

Quite a few recipes in this book call for vegetable stock. Although there are commercially available products, making your own allows you to control the flavors, and ultimately gives much better results. The basic idea is to simmer vegetables in water for a while, then strain them out. The particulars:

Use plenty of onions, they give the most flavor. Four or five medium onions is reasonable for two quarts of stock. More can never hurt. A little less, okay. Peel them and cut them into big chunks.

Use celery and carrots as well. Two or three stalks of celery, and two or three or four carrots is about right for two quarts of broth. Peel or wash the carrots, and cut both the carrots and the celery into chunks. If the celery has leaves, you may as well include them.

A few lightly smashed garlic cloves can't hurt. But they're not strictly necessary.

Unless you're making the broth for something that would benefit from the flavor, don't use mushrooms or tomatoes – they take over, and then you have mushroom broth or tomato broth.

Look at whatever else you have hanging around, and if you think it will help, throw it in. Scallions are good. Parsley, too (adding it for the last five minutes or so, instead of at the beginning, keeps the flavor fresh).

You can scorch the vegetables in a little oil in the stock pot for a while, stirring occasionally, before adding the water. Or not. If you do, you get a darker stock with a richer flavor. If you don't, the flavor is more delicate – also good.

Use one teaspoon of salt per quart of water.

After bringing the stock to a boil, simmer for at least twenty minutes, and up to an hour. Half an hour is a good standard. And you may as well simmer it covered; it uses less energy, and prevents some of the liquid from boiling off. In any case, you will end up with a little less liquid than you added originally.

Vegetable stock keeps in the refrigerator for at least a week, and maybe two, so you may as well make more than you need right away. And any time you bring it to a boil, the clock starts over, so you can extend the shelf life if you have to.

See photo, page 175 (2 quarts of stock, simmering in the pot).

Dinner

Cheddar Ale Sauce

Inspired by the "Rí Rá Irish Pub" in Burlington, Vermont.

The choice of ale has a noticeable effect on this sauce; my preference is for *Newcastle Brown Ale*, but I have enjoyed the results with many other fine beers (including *Guiness Stout* and *Anchor Steam*). I would shy away from the more bitter beers, such as IPAs, as well as the completely tasteless beers (I won't name names); otherwise whatever you have on hand should be fine.

At *Rí Rá* they serve this over french fries; it is also excellent on steamed broccoli, thickly sliced homemade bread (page 129), and sliced apples.

12 oz beer or ale
3 C milk
10 Tbs flour (1/2 C plus 2 Tbs)
6 Tbs oil (1/4 C plus 2 Tbs)
1 1/8 tsps salt
9 oz extra sharp cheddar, grated

Combine the ale and milk in a heavy bottomed saucepan, and cook over medium heat until boiling or nearly so, stirring occasionally. Make a roux with the oil and flour in a larger heavy bottomed saucepan (this is the pan that will ultimately hold the sauce), and cook, stirring, over medium high heat until bubbling. Lower the heat and whisk in the hot liquid *a little at a time* (or it will form lumps). Add the salt and simmer for a few minutes, stirring frequently, while the sauce thickens, then lower the heat as much as possible and stir in the grated cheddar until melted. Serve hot.

Note: You say to yourself, "Self, why is this not in the 'Sauces' chapter?" Good question, and I considered it. But just look at the picture – around here, we call this dinner.

Broccoli Ring
Adapted from the justly famous "Moosewood Cookbook" by Mollie Katzen.

Or you can make it into one big log, or individual pockets, or "strudel" if you use phyllo dough. All of the options are discussed below.

Yield: 4 pockets, 4 strudels, or 1 log or ring – generously serves 4 in all cases.

Filling:

    6 C chopped broccoli (mostly florets)
    1 C chopped onion
    3 Tbs olive oil
    1 C seasoned breadcrumbs
    8 oz extra sharp cheddar, grated
    2 eggs, beaten
    3/4 tsp salt (divided)
    black pepper

Dough:

    1 batch *Turkish Pizza* dough (page 235), and
    olive oil, for brushing

    Or:

    16 sheets of phyllo dough (9 × 14 inches; about 1/2 lb), and
    about 1/2 C melted butter

Heat the olive oil in a large frying pan, and sauté the onion with 1/2 teaspoon of salt until soft. Add the broccoli, sprinkle with the remaining 1/4 teaspoon of salt, and cook for about 5 minutes.

Mix the vegetables with the rest of the filling ingredients in a large bowl.

Butter a large cookie sheet, and preheat the oven to 375°, without convection, with a rack in the middle or just above. Follow the directions for one of the following variations, and in all cases bake for about 30 minutes, until nicely browned.

Note: Replacing some of the broccoli with asparagus makes a nice variation.

To make a ring: Form the dough into a "rope," about 18 inches long. Press together the ends to make a circle, then roll it out into a thin circle with a circle missing from the middle (imagine a flattened doughnut, but big). Spread the filling over the dough, then fold it up and pinch it together, forming a ring. Get some help transferring the ring to a lightly oiled cookie sheet (or slide a pizza peel under it, a cookie sheet over it, and flip). Brush with olive oil, and cut a few slits in the top to let steam escape.

To make a (curved) log: (Easier than a ring, but perhaps a bit less impressive.) Roll the dough into a long, thin rectangle, spread the filling down the middle, and fold up and pinch together the edges. Transfer to a lightly oiled cookie sheet (you will have to curve it to fit), seam side down. Brush with olive oil, and cut a few slits in the top to let steam escape.

To make pockets: Divide the dough into quarters, roll each into a thin rectangle, and divide the filling among them. Fold up the edges and pinch them together, then place, seam-side down, on a lightly oiled cookie sheet. Brush with olive oil, and cut a few slits in the top to let steam escape.

To make strudel: For each strudel, spread a thin layer of melted butter on each of four sheets of phyllo dough, laid one on top of the other. (For general advice about phyllo dough, see the baklava recipe on page 21 – but you need not clarify the butter.) Take 1/4 of the filling and form it into a fat log at one end of the phyllo (across the shorter dimension), leaving about an inch margin on all three adjacent edges. Fold up the inch at the sides first, extending the fold the length of the phyllo sheet.

Then fold up the inch at the bottom, and roll the whole thing up to the far edge. Place the strudel on the cookie sheet with the seam down, and brush it with melted butter. Cut a few thin slits in each strudel to let steam escape.

Cashew Burgers

We are poorer for the dissolution of Brattleboro's *Common Ground* restaurant, where I had my first cashew burger. This recipe evolved from my (failed) attempts to recreate their invention; although it is decidedly different, it is nonetheless delicious, and might even compare favorably should some intrepid time traveler kindly deliver one fresh from the Common Ground for a taste test.

Yield: 8 good-sized burgers.

>2 C raw cashew pieces
>1 C walnuts
>1 medium onion, chopped
>2 C cooked white rice (see notes)
>4 oz sharp cheddar, grated
>1 1/4 tsps salt
>black pepper
>oil

Toast the cashews in a 350° oven (with convection) for about 15 minutes, until golden brown; toast the walnuts for about 10 minutes. Sauté the onion in a little oil until soft.

Lightly oil a large cookie sheet.

Combine the nuts, onion, salt, and a generous amount of black pepper in a food processor, and process until there are no large pieces remaining. Then mix all of the ingredients together. Form into burgers, and arrange these on the cookie sheet.

Preheat the oven to 400°, without convection, with a shelf just above the middle. Just before baking, lightly brush the burgers with oil, then bake for 15 – 20 minutes, until lightly browned.

Serve on rolls with all of the usual trimmings.

Notes:

>If you're using leftover rice, microwave it briefly with a little water to freshen it up a bit – this will help bind the burgers together better.

>I generally use jasmine rice, which has a bit of stickiness to it (and a nice flavor), but any somewhat sticky rice will do (I would avoid basmati).

>If fried in a generous amount of oil the burgers develop a nice crunchy crust, but also absorb a fair amount of the oil. It's a trade-off; you decide. You could also try frying them (in a nonstick pan) with just a smattering of oil, and then perhaps baking them.

Vegetarian Gyro Pockets
Adapted from "Seitan and Beyond" by Skye Michael Conroy.

Served in pita bread with a cucumber-yogurt ("tzatziki") sauce, these are excellent. The gyro must be prepared the day before, so some advance planning is required.

You will need *heavy duty* aluminum foil for baking, preferably the 18 inch wide variety.

Serves 4.

1 1/2 C vital wheat gluten
2 Tbs porcini mushroom powder
1 Tbs dried minced onion
1 Tbs onion powder
1/2 tsp black pepper
1 1/2 C water
3 Tbs tamari
2 Tbs olive oil
2 tsps dried marjoram
1 tsp ground cumin
1 tsp dried oregano
1/2 tsp dried rosemary, crushed
2 Tbs minced or crushed garlic

pita bread (page 140)
cucumber yogurt sauce (page 84), to serve

Preheat the oven to 350°, without convection, with a rack in the middle or just above.

Mix together the vital wheat gluten, porcini mushroom powder, minced and powdered onions, and black pepper in a large bowl. Put all the remaining ingredients except the garlic in a blender, and blend until smooth. Stir the garlic into the blender ingredients (without blending further).

Mix the wet ingredients into the dry with a latex spatula until the mixture is uniform and holds together well, then set aside for 10 minutes, to ensure that all of the liquid is absorbed.

Lay out a large square of aluminum foil and transfer the dough onto it. Form it into a short, thick cylinder, and roll it tightly in the foil, carefully twisting the ends to compact the results. (The foil tears easily, especially while twisting the ends; try to avoid that…). Roll again in a second sheet of foil, also twisting the ends carefully. (One sheet is not enough, and if either sheet tears – even just a little – use a third. The sound of the gyro exploding in the oven is unforgettable, and it makes something of a mess…).

Bake for 2 hours, turning over halfway through. Allow to cool, then refrigerate overnight.

Just before dinner, preheat the oven to 425°, with two racks a few inches apart, more or less in the middle of the oven. Spread some olive oil on two large cookie sheets.

Unwrap the gyro, and cut it in half crosswise, so that each half can stand vertically. Slice the gyro into relatively thin, irregular strips, and spread them in a single layer on the baking sheets (if you can fit them all on one sheet, then you've sliced them too thickly; if two sheets are not enough, too thinly…). Brush them lightly with olive oil, and bake for about 15 minutes, swapping their positions halfway through, until they start to crisp up a bit in places.

Serve in pita bread (page 140) with cucumber yogurt sauce and perhaps some standard salad components (like lettuce, tomato, onion).

Note: Porcini mushroom powder can be hard to find; order it online if you need to, but don't skip it. Ignore the less-than-appealing aroma; have faith.

Fake Chicken with Cashews

Adapted (and in particular, vegetarianized) from "Simple Thai Food" by Leela Punyaratabandhu.

A true family favorite.

Serves 4.

Main Dish:

    1 batch fake chicken (page 199)
    3 Tbs corn starch
    1 medium onion
    3 or 4 scallions
    2 cloves garlic, crushed
    1/2 C water
    2 Tbs oyster sauce
    2 Tbs soy sauce
    2 tsps (packed) brown sugar
    3 or 4 dried Thai red chiles
    8 oz roasted, unsalted whole cashews
    3/4 C oil

    rice, to serve

Extra Sauce:

    1/2 C water
    2 Tbs oyster sauce
    2 Tbs soy sauce
    2 tsps (packed) brown sugar
    1 1/2 tsps corn starch

Dry the "chicken" and cut into bite-sized pieces on the diagonal. Toss with the 3 tablespoons corn starch to coat and set aside.

Cut the onion into wedges through the center, about 1/2 inch wide at the outermost layer. Slice the white parts of the scallions into thin rounds and add them to the onion; cut the green parts into inch long pieces on the diagonal and keep these separate.

Mix together the water, oyster sauce, soy sauce, and brown sugar, and set aside; do the same in a small saucepan for the "extra sauce" (same ingredients, with the addition of corn starch).

Prepare the chiles by cutting them in half and shaking out all the seeds (if necessary, quarter them to get to any difficult to remove seeds, but don't make too many small pieces, because you're going to need to be able to scoop these out of the pan with a slotted spoon).

Heat the oil in your widest pan over medium heat. When the oil is hot, add the cashews, and cook, stirring, until the cashews have browned. Remove them with a slotted spoon, leaving behind as much oil as possible, and drain on a paper towel lined plate.

Add the chiles to the pan and fry for about a minute, then remove these with the slotted spoon and add them to the cashews. Make sure to get every last piece, as anything that remains will burn.

Turn the heat to high, and once the oil is very hot, fry the fake chicken in two batches. Fry each batch for about 4 minutes, turning each piece over once (or twice, for strangely shaped pieces), so that it cooks on all sides. Don't move the pieces around while you're cooking them; let them develop a nice crust. When they're done, remove with a slotted spoon and transfer to another paper towel lined plate to drain.

Bring the extra sauce to a simmer, stirring occasionally, while you complete the last steps. (This is to serve on the side, with the rice.)

Remove all but a thin layer of oil from the pan. With the heat still on high, add the onions, white parts of the scallions, and the garlic, and fry, stirring, until the onions have softened a little, about a minute. Then add the sauce mixture – be careful, it will steam violently – stir, and immediately add the fake chicken, stirring well to coat. Add the cashews and chiles, and the green parts of the scallions, and stir fry for 30 seconds or so. Then transfer to a large bowl and serve.

Notes:

Oyster sauce, surprisingly, actually does have a trace amount of oyster in it. Vegetarian oyster sauce (flavored with mushrooms) is available, and is perfectly suitable.

Avoid using small pieces of cashew, as they are difficult to remove from the pan.

Fake Chicken
Adapted from "Seitan and Beyond" by Skye Michael Conroy.

This recipe gives you the means to adapt a host of traditional chicken dishes (such as the preceding recipe, on page 197) into their vegetarian counterparts.

Yield: About 18 ounces.

    1 C vital wheat gluten
    2 tsps onion powder
    1 tsp garlic powder
    1/2 14 oz block extra firm tofu (see notes)
    1/3 C water
    1 Tbs white miso
    1 Tbs oil
    3/4 tsp salt

    2 or 3 quarts vegetable stock (page 184), for simmering

Preheat the oven to 350°, without convection, with a rack in the middle or just above.

Mix the vital wheat gluten with the onion and garlic powders in a medium sized bowl. Put all of the remaining ingredients in a blender, and puree until perfectly smooth. Stir the tofu mixture into the vital wheat gluten with a rubber spatula, then knead by hand for a few minutes.

Cut the gluten into 24 more or less equal pieces, then work each one into a fat, finger-like strip. Place a metal cooling rack in a large sheet pan, put a piece of parchment paper on top of the cooling rack, and arrange the pieces on the parchment paper. Bake for 20 minutes.

Meanwhile, bring the vegetable stock to a boil in a large, wide pot. When the "chicken" pieces have finished baking, transfer them to the simmering broth, and simmer for 20 minutes, stirring occasionally.

Remove from the heat, cover, and allow to cool for a few hours.

Use a slotted spoon to transfer the pieces to a storage container or plastic bag, add a little of the broth, and refrigerate overnight before using.

Notes:

    Half of a 14 ounce block of tofu doesn't weigh 7 ounces (it weighs more – somehow they figure in the absorbed water). Cut the block in half and call it close enough.

    It's not a lot of extra work to make a double batch, and then you're not left with half a block of tofu that you have to figure out how to use.

    You only need the vegetable stock temporarily, for simmering – you can use it afterwards to make something else.

Bill's Crab Cakes

It looks like a lot of ingredients, but in reality these are mostly crab, with a little something to bind them together, and some spices. The crab predominates, as it should.

I think Bill snagged this recipe from one of those airline magazines, messed with it some, and then I messed with it a little more, but in any case the original source is long forgotten, so Bill gets the credit. Nice job, Bill – these are excellent.

Yield: About 6 decent sized crab cakes.

> 1 lb lump crabmeat
> 1/4 C onion, minced
> 1/4 C red bell pepper, minced
> 1 Tbs olive oil, plus a little more for frying
> 5 Tbs panko bread crumbs
> 1/4 C mayonnaise
> 2 tsps *Old Bay* seasoning
> 1 tsp coarsely ground garlic
> 1 tsp worcestershire sauce
> 1/2 tsp red pepper sauce
> 1/4 tsp celery salt
> 1 tsp fresh lemon juice
> 2 Tbs scallion greens (or chives), minced
> 1 egg yolk, beaten
> 1/4 tsp black pepper

Sauté the red pepper and onion in 1 tablespoon olive oil until soft; set aside.

Combine all of the remaining ingredients except the crab in a mixing bowl. Mix in the red pepper and onion, and then fold in the crab, trying not to break up the pieces. Form into patties.

Preheat the oven to 350°, without convection, with a rack in the middle or just above.

Heat a little olive oil in a wide (preferably nonstick) frying pan; when the oil is good and hot, brown the patties for 2 minutes on each side, and remove to a lightly oiled cookie sheet. When all of the patties have been browned, bake for 5 minutes. Serve immediately.

Notes:

> Use good crabmeat! The kind that they sell refrigerated in plastic containers seems to be the best available – certainly it is better than canned. I suppose that in theory you should

be able to wrest the meat out of actual crabs, and maybe that would be better, but I have no experience in that area and can't say. Refrigerated will be fine.

It's traditional to serve crab cakes with some sort of sauce, "remoulade" being the most common. I have yet to find a sauce that improves the basic crab cake, and so I simply eat mine plain. They are plenty moist, and need nothing else. You are of course welcome and encouraged to experiment with whatever you care to conjure up.

Cold Sesame Noodles

Another classic, and my go-to choice for pot lucks – always popular.

>1 lb udon noodles (dried – not fresh)
>4 Tbs toasted sesame oil, divided
>3 Tbs tamari
>1 Tbs soy sauce
>1 Tbs water
>3 Tbs red wine vinegar
>1 Tbs sugar
>1 1/2 Tbs tahini
>2 Tbs peanut butter
>1 Tbs crushed garlic
>1 1/2 Tbs minced ginger
>about 1/4 tsp cayenne pepper, to taste
>chopped scallion greens, to garnish

Cook the noodles, drain, and run under cold water, mixing by hand, until fully cooled. Transfer to a large mixing bowl, toss with 2 tablespoons of the sesame oil, and set aside.

Combine the tamari, soy sauce, water, vinegar, sugar, tahini, and peanut butter in a small mixing bowl.

Fry the ginger, garlic, and cayenne in the remaining 2 tablespoons of sesame oil over medium low heat for a few minutes – stop before the garlic starts to brown. Remove from heat, stir in the sauce mixture, pour over the noodles, and toss until evenly coated. Garnish with chopped scallions and refrigerate.

Notes:

>Other wheat-based oriental noodles will do – they don't have to be specifically called "udon." But not rice noodles, and don't even *think* about making this with spaghetti…
>
>If you double the recipe, consider cooking the noodles in two batches – I have found that even in my largest pot it's impossible to cook two pounds of udon noodles without having them stick together in undercooked clumps.

Pasta with Crispy Chickpeas

This arose from what we had around the house one night, but now I go out of my way to contrive to have these things around now and then. Good stuff.

Serves 4.

> 2 medium broccoli crowns (about 6 C chopped florets)
> 3 or 4 large cloves garlic, thinly sliced
> 4 or 5 Tbs olive oil, divided
> 1 15 oz can chickpeas
> 1 lb pasta
> 1/2 C grated pecorino romano cheese, plus extra to serve
> 1/2 C sun-dried tomatoes (packed in olive oil), chopped
> 3/4 tsp salt, divided
> 3/4 tsp smoked paprika
> black pepper

Preheat the oven to 375°, with convection, with a rack in the middle or just above.

There is no way around it, crisping the chickpeas is a pain in the buttocks. Rinse them, dry them as well as you can between two towels, and then *you really, absolutely have to remove the skin from each individual chickpea.* Each one. This you do by squeezing the chickpea between two fingers; it will pop out of its skin, which you discard. Do this methodically, working your way through the whole batch (you won't believe how many there are in that one small can), carefully separating the skinned chickpeas from those that still need attention. Once you're done, give them a final drying with a paper towel (the drier they are, the crispier they will become), toss with 1 tablespoon of olive oil and 1/4 teaspoon of salt, spread on a cookie sheet, and bake for 30 – 40 minutes, stirring or shaking once or twice, until they are well browned. When they are done, transfer them to a small bowl and mix them with the smoked paprika and a couple of grinds of black pepper.

Start a large pot of water boiling for the pasta.

Heat 2 tablespoons of olive oil in a large frying pan, and add the garlic. Cook over medium low heat until the garlic browns, then lower the heat, add the broccoli, sprinkle evenly with 1/2 teaspoon of salt (two 1/4 teaspoon additions with some mixing in between is a good method), and cook, stirring occasionally, until the broccoli is relatively tender (use a metal spatula to get the garlic up off the bottom of the pan and into the mix).

Cook the pasta in the boiling water, drain thoroughly, and toss with a little olive oil. Mix in the broccoli, sun-dried tomatoes, and grated cheese, and then finally the crisped chickpeas, and serve immediately, with extra grated cheese on the side.

Notes:

This is an elaborate variation on what is perhaps the dinner I make most frequently – "Pasta with Broccoli and Garlic." Leave out the chickpeas (along with the paprika and extra salt) and sun-dried tomatoes; don't leave out the grated cheese. Simple, healthy, and very popular.

Smoked paprika is *amazing* – a revelation. Please don't substitute ordinary paprika.

It is possible – and admittedly easier – to crisp the chickpeas by simply drying them and frying them in olive oil, but the results are quite greasy, and it makes the dish somewhat indigestible… I don't recommend it.

Garlic Pasta

Inspired by something the "Fantastic Foods" company used to make...

Nutritious, delicious, and just a little bit suspicious. You can make this in the time it takes to boil the pasta, and if you keep some nutritional yeast in the fridge, then chances are you always have the ingredients on hand. A great last minute meal.

> 1 lb pasta
> 1/2 C nutritional yeast
> 2 tsps garlic powder
> 1 tsp salt
> 1/4 C olive oil
>
> Optional: smoked paprika

Boil the pasta in unsalted water.

Mix together the nutritional yeast, garlic powder, and salt.

Drain the pasta, toss first with the olive oil, then with the yeast, garlic, and salt mixture. Serve with smoked paprika.

Macaroni and Cheese

This is not just any macaroni and cheese – there's nothing fancy about it, and yet it is really quite something. You will not be disappointed.

> 1 lb pasta
> 3 1/2 C milk (lowfat is fine)
> 5 Tbs flour
> 4 Tbs oil
> 1 tsp onion powder
> 1 tsp salt
> 10–12 oz extra sharp cheddar cheese, grated
> 1/3 C seasoned breadcrumbs

Grease a 9 × 13 × 2 inch glass casserole, or something similar. Undercook the pasta – about 2/3 of the way to the recommended *al dente* time is about right (it will finish cooking in the oven). Drain, and spread evenly in the casserole.

Preheat the oven to 375°, without convection, with a rack in the upper middle.

Scald the milk over medium heat in a heavy bottomed saucepan, stirring occasionally (it need not boil). When the milk is nearly ready, make the roux: Combine the flour, oil, onion powder, and salt in a saucepan and cook over medium-low heat until it starts to bubble. Turn the heat down to very low and whisk the milk into the roux a little at a time, until it is all added. Add the cheese and stir until it is melted (just a minute or two), and then pour the sauce evenly over the pasta. A little bit of mixing in the casserole is advisable to even things out a bit.

Sprinkle with the breadcrumbs and bake for 35–40 minutes, until bubbly and browned on top.

Notes:

> Elbow macaroni is traditional, but other shapes are fun, too.
>
> If you add too much milk at once to the roux, then the cheese sauce will get lumpy. If that happens you can fix it by blending with an immersion mixer, or in a food processor or blender.

Spinach Ravioli

How to make pasta is a book in itself, and one that I'm not interested in writing. So I am mostly going to assume that you have some experience, or that you're going to research the basics elsewhere (if you need a reference, you can't go wrong with the standard *Essentials of Classic Italian Cooking* by Marcella Hazan).

Yield: About 64 2-inch ravioli.

Pasta:

>   4 eggs
>   About 2 C flour

Filling:

>   16 oz fresh baby spinach
>   1 1/2 C part skim ricotta (drained overnight, if possible)
>   30 g grated pecorino romano
>   2 cloves garlic, crushed
>   2 Tbs olive oil, separated
>   1 1/8 tsps salt
>   a few grinds of black pepper

Prepare the pasta dough: Make a well in the center of 2 cups of flour, add the eggs, and mix with a fork, gradually incorporating flour until the mixture becomes doughy. Knead well; the dough should become strong and smooth. Wrap in plastic and set aside while you prepare the filling.

Rinse the spinach. Heat 1 tablespoon of the olive oil in a large pot over high heat; when the oil is hot add the spinach and cook, stirring, until it's all wilted. Transfer the spinach to a colander, and leave it there to drain and cool.

Meanwhile, sauté the garlic in the remaining 1 tablespoon of olive oil.

When the spinach has cooled enough to handle comfortably, wrap it in a double layer of cheese cloth and squeeze as much water as you can out of it; be aggressive – wring it, twist it, dig your fingers in… Then lay it out on a cutting board and chop it finely.

If the ricotta hasn't drained overnight, wrap it in some cheese cloth as well (you can re-use the piece you used for the spinach) and squeeze some water out of it. Then mix all of the filling ingredients together.

To assemble the ravioli, start by dividing the pasta dough into eight sections. For each one, roll it out thinly (see notes) into a long rectangle, ideally about 4 inches wide (that takes some practice;

if it's wider or narrower, no big deal – make bigger or smaller ravioli). Line one long edge of the rectangle with dollops of filling, each about a slightly rounded teaspoonful, and each about an inch apart and 3/4 of an inch from the edge. Fold the other long edge over the filling, and seal the ravioli, working your way from one end to the other, by first pressing down the pasta between the mounds of filling, and then pressing down where the two edges meet. As you do so, try to squeeze out as much air as you can. Once they are all sealed, cut the ravioli apart, either with a knife or a fluted pastry cutter. Place the completed ravioli on a dishtowel (in a cookie sheet to facilitate relocation), not touching each other.

Do this to each of the eight sections of pasta in turn – finish filling one before starting to roll the next, so that the pasta doesn't start to dry until after you've filled it. Keep the dough you aren't using wrapped in plastic until you're ready for it.

To cook, get a large pot of water boiling, carefully add the ravioli (you should be able to "pour" them out of their towels directly into the water), and boil gently for 4 or 5 minutes or so – the cooking time will depend to some degree on how long the ravioli have been sitting out drying; you can bite into an edge to test for doneness, if you like. Remove with a strainer or large slotted spoon (if you must pour them into a colander, be careful…), and toss gently with a little olive oil to keep them from sticking to each other.

Notes:

> How thin you roll the pasta will of course have a significant effect on both the quality and the quantity of your results. My pasta maker, a *Marcato* brand *Atlas 150*, has thicknesses from 1 (the thickest) to 9; I roll it to a 7.

> It's a mistake to use water to seal the edges – they'll seal fine without it, and it makes it harder to squeeze out the air. Just make sure to press down on the edges before cutting.

> If the ravioli are going to sit for a while before you cook them, turn them over now and then so that the tops and bottoms dry evenly.

> It goes a lot faster with a helper – one person rolls, the other fills. (Plus, it gives you someone to blame if any of them fall apart.)

Pasta with Roasted Cauliflower

1 lb pasta
1 head cauliflower
1/4 C plus 1 Tbs olive oil, divided
1/2 C seasoned breadcrumbs
1/2 C grated pecorino romano cheese, plus more for serving
1/4 tsp crushed red pepper
1/2 tsp salt
a few grinds of black pepper
chopped parsley

Preheat the oven to 475° (with convection), with a shelf at the very bottom. Start a large pot of water heating on the stove for the pasta.

Cut the cauliflower into small florets, and toss with 1/4 cup olive oil and the salt and black pepper. Spread onto a large cookie sheet, and tent tightly with aluminum foil. Bake for 10 minutes, then remove the foil, stir, and return to the oven (without replacing the foil) for another 10 minutes. Stir once more, and return to the oven for a final baking of 8 – 10 minutes.

While the cauliflower is baking, sauté the red pepper flakes in the remaining 1 tablespoon olive oil for a minute or two, then add the breadcrumbs and stir until crisped and slightly darkened.

Salt the boiling water and cook the pasta, then toss with the cauliflower, grated cheese, breadcrumbs, and parsley. Serve with extra grated cheese.

Spinach Calzone

Always popular. You can make them any size; I make mine on the small side, so there are more to go around, but do as you see fit.

Yield: 12 calzones; serves about 6.

> 2 × the usual pizza dough recipe (page 151)
>
> 2 cloves garlic, crushed
> 1 medium onion, chopped
> 1 Tbs olive oil
> 11 oz fresh baby spinach
> 1 lb ricotta
> 8 oz mozzarella, grated
> 1.5 oz pecorino romano, grated
> 3/4 tsp salt
>
> extra olive oil, for brushing

Prepare the pizza dough as instructed in the recipe, but leave it to rise as one large ball. When you are ready to begin preparing the filling, divide the dough into 12 equal pieces (fewer, if you want to make larger calzones), form each into a ball, and set aside on a floured surface, covered with a dishtowel, and then with plastic wrap.

Sauté the onion and garlic in the olive oil until the onion is soft and translucent. Cook the spinach in a large pot over high heat, stirring, until it is thoroughly wilted. Press out as much water as you can with the back of a wooden spoon in a metal sieve, or else by wrapping the spinach in cheese cloth and wringing it out (rubber dishwashing gloves help if the spinach is hot; there is also the option of letting it cool a few minutes first…). Once the spinach is drained, transfer it to a cutting board and chop it up a bit.

Lightly oil a large cookie sheet. Preheat the oven to 425°, without convection, with a rack in the middle or just above.

Mix together all the filling ingredients. Weigh the filling, and determine how much will go in each calzone. Weigh out the filling for one calzone, and let that guide how you roll your first dough ball (on a lightly floured surface) – about 5 inches in diameter is about right, if you're making 12. Fill a small bowl with water, and lightly dampen one edge of the dough with your finger, then pull up the edges and pinch them together. Use the back of a fork to press the edges together even more firmly. Place the calzone on the prepared tray, and start the next one. Leave a little space between them, and when the tray is full, brush each calzone with olive oil, and cut a small slit in the top to allow steam to escape – make sure to get all the way through to the filling, and wiggle the knife slightly to make sure the slit doesn't close up. Don't try to fit them all on one tray; accept that there will be a second batch.

Bake for about 15 minutes, until golden brown. Allow to cool for a few minutes before serving, or else cut them in half and let them cool on plates – they are very hot inside…

Notes:

> These days they sell ricotta in 15 ounce containers, which should be prosecuted as a crime against humanity. But okay, if you're only making one batch, that will do. For some reason, the larger containers are still 32 ounces – 2 pounds – so if you're doubling the recipe, you can use the full amount.
>
> Similarly, 11 ounces just happens to be the currently popular size of a container of fresh baby spinach; if you have a little more or less, fine. And it doesn't have to be "baby" spinach – full grown, adult spinach works just as well, but there's a little extra work to do in removing the stems.
>
> Look, the cheese is going to get out, there is no way around it. Cutting slits in the top is my way of trying to control where and how it gets out, and it works pretty well. Occasionally some will burst through a side or a seam, which is less attractive, but still delicious – don't take it personally; it happens. As with so many other minor culinary defects, no one will complain.
>
> Making fewer, larger calzones would be a little less work – no way to deny it. I still make 12, but I may switch to 8 one of these days.

Black Tofu

This recipe is *very* heavily adapted – as in barely recognizable – from Ottolenghi's "Black Pepper Tofu" in his book *Plenty*. No offense to the chef, but if you follow his recipe, the result is *inedible*. Five *tablespoons* of crushed black pepper – it's like eating sand.

In any case, Ottolenghi's tofu was tasty enough to get me working on an edible version (delicious, even), and here it is. It requires the procurement of three very specific varieties of Asian soy sauce; if you can't get them (try an oriental grocery), make something else – they're the key. The first, "kecap manis," is also known as Indonesian "sweet soy sauce." The others are Chinese "light" and "dark" soy sauces; don't try to substitute the more common Japanese variety.

As far as the other ingredients are concerned, shallots are good, but if you don't have them, onion will suffice. And if you don't have onion, that's okay too – it's fine to leave it out altogether. Same for the scallions – a nice touch, but not essential. If you have a little ginger and/or garlic lying around and feel like adding it, then sure, throw it in, it can't hurt. But it won't make much of a difference; it's all about the sauce. Don't tell Ottolenghi, but if you omit the pepper entirely, it's also okay.

2 14 oz packages extra firm tofu
2 Tbs plus 2 tsp sugar
1 Tbs plus 1 tsp corn starch
1 tsp crushed black pepper
6 Tbs kecap manis (Indonesian sweet soy sauce)
3 Tbs Chinese light soy sauce
2 Tbs plus 2 tsp Chinese dark soy sauce
2 or 3 medium shallots, sliced thinly
2 or 3 scallions, green parts only, chopped
additional corn starch for dusting tofu
oil for frying

rice for serving

Drain the tofu blocks by placing them on an inclined cutting board (put a bunched up dish towel under one end) with a heavy cutting board on top.

While the tofu drains, make the sauce. Stir together the sugar, corn starch, and black pepper in a small mixing bowl, then add the three soy sauces and mix.

Cut each block of tofu into 24 cubes (halve the block along the shortest dimension, quarter it along the longest, and cut it into thirds along the remaining one). Arrange these on a double layer of paper towels, with a paper towel on top, to dry for another 10 or 15 minutes.

Heat about 1/4 inch of oil in a large frying plan. Put the tofu cubes in a plastic bag (a grocery store produce bag is ideal), and add 2 or 3 tablespoons of corn starch, one tablespoon at a time, closing the bag and shaking to distribute the corn starch evenly between additions. When the oil is hot, fry the tofu in small batches, turning each piece over once. The tofu should end up golden brown on all sides. Drain briefly on paper towels before transferring to a large mixing bowl.

When all of the tofu has been fried, pour the hot oil into a *completely dry*, metal or *pyrex* receptacle for recycling or disposal. (If it's not *completely dry*, any droplets of water will *explode* when the hot oil hits them (ask me how I know…). If it's glass but not *pyrex*, it may very well shatter.) Leave the pan off the heat for a couple of minutes or so to cool down, then add a little of the oil back to just coat the bottom, and add the shallots. You might not even have to turn the burner on right away. Fry the shallots, stirring often, until they are soft and a little bit browned. When the shallots are ready, give the sauce a quick stir (the corn starch and sugar will likely have settled), add it to the hot pan, and cook, stirring, for about a minute, until the sauce thickens.

Pour the sauce over the tofu and toss until all the pieces are coated. Add the scallions, mix briefly, and transfer to a serving bowl (or serve in the mixing bowl if you're not being fancy).

Serve over rice.

Roasted Tofu

This is a basic marinated tofu recipe. The marinade is sufficient for two 14 oz. blocks, provided you follow the very clever instructions below…

Yield: 16 pieces.

>   2 14 oz blocks of firm or extra firm tofu
>   1/2 C soy sauce
>   1/2 C red wine or water
>   1 Tbs brown sugar
>   1 Tbs toasted sesame oil
>   minced fresh ginger
>   minced or crushed garlic
>   1/2 tsp crushed red pepper flakes

Open the tofu packages, pressing what water can be easily removed from the blocks, and *reserve the packages* – these are your marinating containers.

Place a dish towel under one end of a cutting board, set the blocks of tofu on the board, and place a heavy cutting board (or a cutting board with a weight on it) on top of the tofu blocks. Allow to drain like this for 15 or 20 minutes or so.

Mix the marinade ingredients together in a small bowl.

Cut each block of tofu into 8 slabs.

Put a tablespoon or two of marinade in the bottom of each tofu package. Return the cut tofu to the packages, and pour the marinade evenly over the tofu. Use a butter knife to separate the pieces, ensuring that the marinade seeps into the spaces between the slabs. Refrigerate for at least an hour.

Transfer to a lightly oiled cookie sheet, and bake in the upper half of the oven at 375°, with convection, for about 45 minutes, turning the pieces over halfway through. Serve hot or cold.

Becky's Potatonik

Becky, my great grandmother, learned to make this from her mother, who learned from her mother, who learned from hers, and on and on. I learned from Becky, who was amused that a boy wanted to cook, but kindly indulged me, as always. Becky had no "recipe;" what follows is based on the notes I took as a teenager, and the adjustments I've made over the intervening decades. But for the record, Becky's original instructions included adding flour until the batter was "loose but not too loose," and letting it rise "a long time." That's the way it used to be done, my friends.

Becky also used long, thin metal pans that had been passed down through the generations and were well seasoned, and she greased them liberally with shortening. Unless you are fortunate enough to have your great grandmother's potatonik pans, removing a baked potatonik from a loaf pan can be an unparalleled exercise in frustration (and destruction), and I offer some of my more successful ideas below.

Finally, Becky had four sons, each of whom married and had children of their own, and the entire clan came to visit every weekend. When Becky made potatonik, she started with ten pounds of potatoes, and had the oven going all day. I have cut it down to five pounds, which I can bake in two batches, but if you wanted to get out of the kitchen sooner, you could certainly cut it in half again. But you can never have too much potatonik.

Yield: 8 loaves.

> 5 lbs russet potatoes
> 2 C warm water
> 3 1/2 tsps yeast
> 3 eggs, lightly beaten
> 1/2 C oil
> 1 Tbs salt
> 20 oz flour
>
> Optional (but recommended): onion, sliced into 1/8 inch rings

Peel the potatoes, and ideally grind them in a meat grinder (but if that's not possible, shred them coarsely using a box grater; the shredding disk on your food processor would probably also do fine). The potatoes will release quite a bit of water during this process; you want it all – everything goes into the batter. Transfer the ground potatoes to a very large mixing bowl; a very large pot works well, too (and if it has a lid, even better). The batter will rise significantly, so make sure there is plenty of extra room.

Dissolve the yeast in the water, and mix into the potatoes. Mix in the eggs, oil, and salt. Stir in the flour, a cup or so at a time, until the batter is "loose but not too loose" – the full 20 ounces should be just about right, but you are welcome to use your own judgment. Cover and let rise for 3 to 4 hours.

Preheat the oven to 400°, without convection, with a rack in the middle or just above.

Prepare four loaf pans… You could grease them liberally with shortening; this works well enough, though you will still have some wrestling to do to get them out of the pans, and the results will be a bit greasy – delicious, but when you eat too many of them (which you will), you will feel it.

Teflon (and maybe other nonstick) pans, by the way, work like a charm, lightly greased with butter or shortening, *the very first time they are used.* After that, no – the miracle is over.

I have had some luck buttering and then flouring my pans; that works passably well (but not perfectly – you will certainly have some work to do to release them, and you will undoubtedly wreck a few – which is okay, those are traditionally eaten before they ever make it to the table…).

And then there's parchment paper. This is my top choice. Commune with your inner origamist, and fold a piece of parchment paper to fit in the bottom of each loaf pan. (You can start by turning the pan upside down and folding the parchment paper over its outside, if that makes it easier.) It doesn't have to be perfect. Trim the edges (or at least the edge that will be in front) to the height of the pan, so that you can see how the potatonik is cooking through the oven window, without having to open the oven door.

Once your pans are prepared and your oven is preheated, lay some onion rings in the bottom of each pan, if you like (these are optional, but good!), give the potatonik batter a quick stir, and transfer it to the pans using a ladle until it is somewhere between 1/2 and 3/4 of an inch deep. Put these in the oven, and bake until the potatonik is deeply browned, which generally takes between an hour and 15 minutes and an hour and a half.

Release the loaves from the pans, wash and prepare them for the next batch, and go to it again. (If you've used parchment paper, no washing is necessary, but I do recommend fresh pieces of parchment paper.)

Potatonik should be served warm, sliced crosswise into rectangles. Some people put butter on theirs, which I never understood, but I mention it anyway because once there was something I didn't understand that made sense anyway (I can't think of what it might have been, though). If you're not serving it directly from the oven, it reheats well in a toaster-oven (or oven), just briefly so it doesn't dry out; it would be a *shanda* – a travesty or a scandal, in Yiddish – to let it anywhere near a microwave.

Note: The astute among you will realize that the second batch rises quite a bit longer than the first; no worries, it's all good. Becky baked hers all day, batch after batch, and nobody ever complained that one batch was inferior to another.

Mashed Potato Casserole

Start with your best, well-seasoned mashed potatoes, leftover or otherwise. Grate some cheese (cheddar is good), and chop some scallions. Mix some of the cheese into the potatoes.

Heat a cast iron pan in a 400° oven for at least 10 minutes, then take it out and swirl a chunk of butter around in it. Transfer the mashed potatoes to the pan, top with the cheese and scallions, and bake for about 20 minutes.

Vegetarian Pastelón

Pastelón is a Latin American "plantain lasagna," traditionally made with ground beef and commercial seasonings that don't skimp on the monosodium glutamate. My version uses vegetarian "protein crumbles" (derived from TVP – texturized vegetable protein) and natural spices. The result is quite delicious and certainly unusual, at least for the average American palate.

A "ripe" plantain is significantly more black than yellow, and can be challenging to peel. Experts recommend lengthwise scoring with a sharp paring knife; in my experience that's a good start, but may still be followed by an unpleasant struggle. And color is not the whole story; I have encountered plantains that looked the same but varied greatly in ripeness. In short, I have quite honestly not really figured these things out yet… But that hasn't stopped me from cooking with them anyway, and neither should it stop you – take a shot, this meal is worth it.

- 4 ripe plantains
- 1 lb vegetarian protein crumbles
- 1 onion, chopped
- 1 green pepper, chopped
- 3 cloves garlic, crushed
- 1 1/2 tsps salt
- 2 1/2 tsps oregano
- 1/2 tsp paprika
- 3/4 tsp coriander
- 1/2 tsp cumin
- 3/4 tsp onion powder
- 3/4 tsp garlic powder
- 1/4 tsp cayenne pepper
- 1/2 C tomato sauce
- 2 eggs
- 2 Tbs milk
- 2 C grated monterey jack cheese

Peel the plantains and slice them lengthwise into 1/4 inch strips – you should get four or five slices per plantain. Coat the bottom of a wide, nonstick pan generously with oil, and fry the plantain slices, four or five at a time, over medium heat for a few minutes on each side, until browned. Drain them briefly on paper towels before transferring to a plate.

When the plantains are all fried, preheat the oven to 350°, with convection, with a rack in the upper middle. Remove all but a tablespoon or two of oil from the pan, and sauté the onions and green pepper. After a few minutes add the garlic; a minute or two later add the veggie crumbles and spices, and then the tomato sauce. Cook for another minute or two, and then remove from the heat.

Butter an 8 inch square pan. The pastelón will have two layers of filling sandwiched between three layers of plantains and cheese. So: layer the bottom with about a third of the plantains, top with half the filling, and then a third of the cheese. Repeat this for the second layer, and then top that with the remaining third of the plantains followed by the remaining third of the cheese.

Mix together the eggs and milk, and pour evenly over the pastelón. Let it sit for a couple of minutes for the custard to seep in, then bake for 20 minutes. Finally, give it a short stay under the broiler to finish it up. Let sit for a few minutes before serving.

Note: The protein crumbles are sold in 12 ounce packages, so you will need two. You can fry up the leftover half pound with some spices to make tasty tacos.

Saag Paneer

In the nearly inconceivable event that you are unfamiliar, this is the famous Indian spinach and cheese dish. It is possible to make your own paneer (Indian cheese), but it's a nontrivial undertaking, and I recommend buying it (at your friendly neighborhood Indian grocery) instead. (If you do make your own, make sure to use milk that isn't "ultra-pasteurized" – cheap milk, essentially. The top quality organic milks will not work.) My goal here has been to recreate the dish as commonly found in restaurants in the U.S.; it seems that this is not authentically Indian. So be it.

Serves 4.

> 14 oz paneer
> 20 oz frozen spinach
> 1 medium onion, chopped
> 2 Tbs fresh ginger, minced
> 2 cloves garlic, crushed
> 1 medium green chile, seeded and minced
> 2 1/2 tsps garam masala
> 1/2 tsp turmeric
> 3/4 tsp salt
> 3/4 C yogurt
> oil, for frying
>
> rice, for serving

Cut the paneer into cubes and fry in small batches in a little oil *in a nonstick pan* over medium low heat, turning each piece so that it browns on four sides. Set aside on a paper towel lined plate.

Microwave the spinach until it's completely defrosted. Use a wire strainer to briefly press out some of the water (but no need to go crazy about it; we will be adding water back in later).

Heat 2 tablespoons of oil in a large frying pan. Add the onion and cook over medium heat, stirring frequently, for 5 to 10 minutes, then add the ginger and cook for another 5 minutes. (If it starts to stick to the bottom, add a little water.) Add the green chile and cook about two minutes more, then add the garlic and cook another two or three minutes. Mix in the garam masala, turmeric, and salt, and cook another minute.

Transfer the spinach to a food processor or blender, and add the onion mixture. Add a little water (maybe half a cup, depending on how aggressively the spinach was drained), and puree.

Return the saag to the pan, heat briefly, stir in the yogurt, and gently mix in the paneer. Serve over rice.

Notes:

I strongly suspect that Indian restaurants use cream, not yogurt. I'm not a fan of cream, and so have substituted yogurt. It works, though it does add a hint of sourness.

Also, Indian restaurants do not commonly fry the paneer. But, as with most things, it really is better fried…

I specify 14 oz. of paneer because it's generally sold in blocks of that weight; nobody ever complained that there was too much paneer in the saag, if you want to use more.

What constitutes "garam masala" is open to interpretation – it's a mix of spices, and brands differ.

Shrimp Etouffee

My version of the New Orleans classic; truly delicious.

Serves 4.

    2 lbs small shrimp (26–30 or 31–35 shrimp per pound) – *with shells*
    3/4 C finely chopped onion
    1/2 C finely chopped celery
    1/2 C finely chopped green pepper
    1/2 C finely chopped scallions
    1 1/2 Tbs minced or crushed garlic
    1/2 C oil
    1/4 C flour
    1 1/2 C shrimp stock (recipe follows)
    2 Tbs sherry
    4 tsp creole seasoning, divided (recipe follows)
    1 1/4 tsps salt
    3 Tbs minced parsley

    cooked white rice (to serve)

Peel the shrimp (save the shells for the stock) and toss with 1 1/2 teaspoons of the creole seasoning.

Make a roux with the oil and flour, and cook over medium heat until bubbling. Add the onion, celery, green pepper, scallions, and garlic, and stir briefly. Add the stock, a little at a time, stirring well, and then the sherry. Bring to a simmer, then lower the heat and simmer for about 10 minutes to thicken the sauce and cook the vegetables. Add the remaining 2 1/2 teaspoons of creole seasoning and the salt. Add the shrimp, turning the heat up to high (to compensate for the cold shrimp). Cook, stirring, for about 5 minutes, lowering the heat somewhat when the etouffee returns to a boil, until the shrimp are done. Remove from the heat, stir in the parsley, and serve over rice.

Notes:

    The onion and celery can be coarsely chopped and then pulsed (separately) in a food processor; not so for the green pepper or scallions (they turn to mush).

    The recipe scales up easily, so is a good choice for a big party.

    A vegetarian version can be made using fake chicken (page 199) and vegetable stock (page 184); decrease the salt to about 3/4 teaspoon to account for the salt content of the stock.

Shrimp Stock:

    shells from 2 lbs shrimp
    1/2 C onion, coarsely chopped
    1/4 C celery, coarsely chopped
    2 garlic cloves, partially smashed
    juice of half a lemon
    1/2 tsp whole black peppercorns

Put all the ingredients in a saucepan and cover with 6 cups of water. Bring to a boil, simmer for 45 minutes, then strain.

Note: This makes about 4 cups – significantly more than you'll need for the etouffee.

Creole Seasoning:

    5 parts paprika
    3 parts salt
    3 parts garlic powder
    2 parts onion powder
    2 parts oregano
    1 part basil
    1 part thyme
    1 part black pepper
    1 part white pepper
    1/2 part cayenne pepper

Mix everything together.

Note: If you make each "part" 1/4 teaspoon, then you'll have a little more than you need for the shrimp etouffee. Or you could mix up more and have it ready the next time you make etouffee; it's also a good general seasoning mix for the likes of fish tacos.

Mujadara
Adapted from "Vegetarian Cooking for Everyone" by Deborah Madison.

Middle Eastern rice and lentils with caramelized onions; a delicious staple. Stuffed into pita (page 140) and topped with tahini yogurt sauce (page 84) it's even better.

    3 or 4 medium onions, sliced
    6 Tbs olive oil
    4 C water
    1 1/4 C lentils (the usual brown variety – nothing fancy), rinsed
    1 1/4 tsps salt
    3/4 C rice, rinsed
    black pepper

Caramelize the onions in the olive oil in a wide pan until they are a very deep brown. (This is easy to say, but tricky to do – if the pan isn't hot enough, or you've been overly generous with the quantity of onions, it will take forever. On the other hand, turn the heat up enough to get the job done, and some of the onions will start to burn before others color at all. All I can tell you is that you can do it; stir a lot (not constantly), and have patience. Sit on a comfortable stool.)

When the onions are done or nearly so, put the lentils and water in a large saucepan, add the salt, and bring to a boil. Turn the heat down and simmer for 20 minutes, then mix in the rice and some black pepper. Cover tightly, and simmer over low heat for 15 minutes, or until the water is fully absorbed. Remove from the heat, stir in the caramelized onions, and let sit for 5 minutes before serving.

Turkish Pizza

Adapted from *The Essential Mediterranean Cookbook* by Whitecap Books (no listed author…), this is not a pizza at all, and traditionally made with lamb; my version is vegetarian.

Serves 4 (two "pizzas" each).

Dough:

>158 g warm water (2/3 C)
>1 tsp yeast
>1/2 tsp sugar
>1 Tbs olive oil
>225 g flour
>3/4 tsp salt

Filling:

>2 Tbs olive oil
>1 medium onion (about 6 oz), finely chopped
>12 oz vegetable protein crumbles
>2 small cloves garlic, crushed
>10 oz canned chopped tomatoes (with juice)
>1 Tbs tomato paste
>3/4 tsp cumin
>1/2 tsp cinnamon
>1/4 tsp cayenne pepper
>1/2 tsp salt
>2 Tbs chopped cilantro
>1/3 C pine nuts
>
>yogurt and additional cilantro, for serving

You can make the dough in a stand mixer, or knead it by hand. In either case, start by sprinkling the yeast onto the warm water, mixing in the sugar, then adding the olive oil and about half the flour. Mix in the salt, and then either gradually add flour, kneading when the dough gets suitably dense, or switch to the dough hook, add almost all of the remaining flour, and let the stand mixer do its thing (use the last bit of flour to finish the dough by hand). Put the dough in an oiled bowl, cover with plastic, and let rise for about an hour.

While the dough is rising, make the filling. In a small bowl, mix together the garlic, tomato paste, tomatoes, spices, and salt, and set aside. Sauté the onions in the olive oil over medium heat in a large, wide pan until soft. Add the veggie crumbles (you can break them up by kneading the package a bit before opening it) and continue to cook another minute or so. Add the tomato and spice mixture, and cook for another 10 to 15 minutes, stirring frequently, so that the filling dries out somewhat. Remove from the heat, mix in the cilantro and half of the pine nuts, and set aside.

Preheat the oven to 425°, without convection, with a rack in the middle or just above. Lightly grease a large cookie sheet with olive oil.

Divide the dough into 8 pieces, and roll each into an oval, about 4 inches by 6 inches. Place 1/8 of the filling on each oval, leaving the sides free. Sprinkle the remaining pine nuts over the pizzas, and fold them up into boat shapes, pinching the two ends together. Place these on the baking tray, and brush the exposed parts of the dough with olive oil. Bake for about 15 minutes, until nicely browned. Serve with yogurt and additional chopped cilantro.

Notes:

You can certainly make fewer, larger, pizzas if you prefer.

I choose my vegetable protein crumbles from the one available brand, *LightLife*…

The dough is on the small size for the stand mixer; you might have to give it a few encouraging stirs with a wooden spoon to encourage to the dough to catch onto the dough hook.

Vegetable Fried Rice
Adapted from "www.gimmesomeoven.com."

This is what you do with leftover rice – in fact, whenever you make something with rice, make extra, so that you can make this.

More guidelines than recipe, the amounts will depend on how much rice you have. Don't measure, wing it. And consider all of the ingredients optional except the rice… (But the peanuts make a big difference, as do the eggs. And the broccoli. Onions and garlic, *of course*. And the peas…)

    about 4 C cooked rice (*cold*)
    1/2 C raw peanuts
    3 eggs
    2 medium carrots, sliced into coins
    1 small onion, chopped
    2 cloves garlic, crushed
    1 medium crown broccoli, cut into florets
    1/2 red bell pepper, chopped
    1/2 C frozen peas
    2 or 3 scallions
    3 – 4 Tbs soy sauce
    2 tsps oyster sauce
    1/2 tsp toasted sesame oil
    butter
    oil
    salt
    black pepper

First prepare all the ingredients. Those things that go in at the same time can share bowls – the carrots, onions, and garlic; the broccoli and red pepper. Everything else gets its own bowl.

Lightly beat the eggs with a pinch or two of salt.

Slice the dark green parts of the scallions on the diagonal; slice the white parts into thin rounds and add those to the onion bowl (save the light green parts for your next vegetable stock).

Heat a wide pan with some height (deeper than a frying pan) over a medium high heat, add a little oil, and roast the peanuts, stirring frequently at first, then constantly as they start to color. Once they've browned, remove them to a bowl and set aside.

Add a little more oil to the pan and a small pat of butter, and pour in the eggs. Give them a few seconds to begin to set, then stir them with a thin metal spatula, cutting them into pieces as you do. As soon as they're cooked through, remove them to a bowl and set aside.

Add yet more oil and butter to the pan, and add the onions, garlic, and carrots, along with a pinch or two of salt and a couple of grinds of black pepper. Stir for about 2 minutes, then add the broccoli and red pepper, and continue to cook, stirring. After another 2 minutes, add the frozen peas, and cook for another minute, still stirring.

Clear some space in the center of the pan, add some more butter and oil, and turn the heat up a little higher. Add the rice, stir fry it for a minute (mixing it in with the vegetables, and actively breaking up clumps), then add the soy sauce (whether you add 3 tablespoons or 4 depends on how much rice you have – does it seem to be less or more than 4 cups?) and the oyster sauce. Mix in the scallions, and cook for about a minute more.

Remove from the heat, stir in the sesame oil, and then the peanuts and eggs, and serve.

Note: If you need it to be truly vegetarian, make sure to use a vegetarian oyster sauce (flavored with mushrooms).

Saffron Rice Pilaf

If you use basmati rice, the grains stay separate after cooking; jasmine rice clumps together a bit. Both are excellent.

> 1 1/2 C rice, preferably basmati or jasmine
> 2 C water
> 3/4 tsp salt
> 1 small onion, chopped finely
> 1/4 C golden raisins
> generous pinch of saffron
> 1/2 C raw (unsalted) pistachios
> oil

Rinse the rice. If using basmati rice, soak it for about 30 minutes before cooking.

Sauté the onion in a little oil in a heavy bottomed saucepan with a tight fitting lid. Once the onion is thoroughly cooked, stir in the rice, and cook, stirring, for a minute or two. Add the water, salt, saffron, and raisins, cover, and bring to a boil. Lower the heat, and simmer gently for about 20 minutes, until all of the water is absorbed.

While the rice is simmering, sauté the pistachios briefly in a little oil.

Once the rice is cooked, fluff it with a fork, mix in the pistachios, cover, and let sit for 5 minutes before serving.

Note: Edward Espe Brown, in his excellent book "Tassajara Cooking," describes how to *listen* to rice – put your ear up close, and you can hear the water bubbling. A little later, when the water is absorbed, you hear nothing. And a little later than that, as the rice on the bottom starts to burn, you hear crackling… You'll need a quiet kitchen. Try to catch it before the crackling, but if not, no worries – just don't scrape the rice from the bottom of the pot.

Becky's Varenikas

Technically, in Russia or the Ukraine, these are "vareniki," but here in the New World, Becky called them "varenikas," so that's what they are. In Poland they call them "pierogi," the only difference being that pierogi are sometimes fried after boiling; varenikas, never (apparently the name comes from the Ukrainian word for "boiled").

A little research shows that many recipes call for some dairy product in the dough – buttermilk, yogurt, sour cream, or kefir (a Russian fermented milk drink); these purportedly make the dough lighter, but why would you want to do that? As written below, the dough is dense and chewy. Yum.

Yield: About 40.

Dough:

> 2 1/2 C flour, plus a little for kneading
> 1 1/2 tsps salt
> 1 egg
> 2/3 C water

Filling:

> 1 1/2 lbs russet potatoes
> 1 medium onion
> 1/4 C oil
> 1 tsp salt

First make the dough: mix the dry and wet ingredients separately, then combine them, knead lightly (you can use a little bit more flour), and cover in plastic wrap. The dough will be a bit sticky. Set this aside while you make the filling.

Peel the potatoes and cut them into chunks, then place them in a pot of water, bring to a boil, and cook until they're soft. While they're cooking, chop the onion and sauté in the oil until translucent, then – optionally – grind them in a food processor or blender. Once the potatoes are done, drain and mash them (preferably with a food mill or potato ricer), and mix with the onion and the salt.

Set a wire rack in a cookie sheet, and cover it with a dish towel – this is where you'll put the varenikas as you complete them. (The wire rack allows some drying from below; it's not strictly necessary, but will make them a little easier to handle. The cookie sheet is also not essential, but it makes it easy to relocate the varenikas if you need to. The dish towel is important! – the varenikas will stick horribly to anything that doesn't breathe.)

To form the varenikas, take about 1/4 or 1/3 of the dough, dust it with flour, and roll it out on a floured surface until it's about 1/16 of an inch thick, or maybe a little less. (Don't make it too thin; the dough should have some bite to it when they're done.) Use a glass with a diameter of 3 1/4 to 3 1/2 inches or so to cut out as many circles as you can. Save the scraps in a piece of plastic wrap; when you run out of dough, you can give these a quick knead and roll the result out to make more. (Just do this once; the dough gets stiffer and drier from repeated flouring and rolling.)

Drop about a teaspoon and a half of filling into the center of one of the circles, then press the edges together around the filling. If you have to stretch the dough a little, fine, but try to stretch the edges of the dough, not the center – the edges are going to be doubled up anyway when you seal them, so they can afford to thin out a bit, the center can't. If you have to stretch the dough more than a little, then you've used too much filling.

If the edges of the dough, where you're going to seal it, are dry and floury, dip your finger in a bowl of water and spread just a little bit on one edge (*only* – two wet edges don't seal so well).

Once you've sealed the edges, go around again, pressing the edge between your thumb and forefinger, from one corner to the other. When you're done, place the finished varenika on the dish towel you've set aside for that purpose, making sure that it doesn't touch any of its neighbors – where they touch, they will assuredly stick.

When you're ready to cook the varenikas, get a large pot of water boiling, and add the varenikas *one at a time* to the pot. (If you try to add them in bulk, you are going to end up with one large varenika, and when you try to pull it apart, it will separate everywhere but where you want it to. Ask me how I know…)

Boil them for about 5 minutes, and then remove them to a serving bowl with a strainer or large slotted spoon. (If you must pour them into a colander, try to do it gently.) Stir in a little olive oil or butter to keep them from sticking, and serve with sour cream.

Note: See also the photograph on page 185 (varenikas boiling in the pot).

Vegetable Pot Pies

Although I still call it "pot pie," I tend to make this more often as a casserole. If you want to go to the extra trouble, you can make individual servings in oven-proof bowls by cutting the phyllo dough to fit each bowl. Otherwise, sheets of phyllo topping a rectangular casserole dish works fine.

Serves 4.

8 C chopped vegetables, including:

>   2 carrots
>   1 or 2 celery stalks
>   broccoli
>   cauliflower

For the sauce:

>   3 C milk
>   5 Tbs oil
>   6 Tbs flour
>   3 tsps onion powder
>   3/4 tsp thyme
>   1/2 tsp black pepper
>   1 1/2 – 1 3/4 tsps salt
>   3 oz extra sharp cheddar, grated

Topping:

>   10 sheets phyllo dough (about 1/4 lb)
>   1/4 – 1/3 C butter, melted

Scald the milk – it need not boil – with the carrots and celery. Make a roux with the oil, flour, and spices, heat it just to bubbling, then turn the heat to low and gradually whisk in the milk. Stir to thicken for a minute or two, then add the salt and cheese, remove from the heat, and stir until the cheese melts. Pour the sauce over the vegetables, mix, and either pour into a 9 × 13 × 2 inch glass baking dish, or divide among oven-proof bowls.

Preheat the oven to 350°, without convection, with a rack in the middle or just above.

Top the casserole or bowls with the phyllo dough, spreading a thin layer of melted butter on each sheet. Use a sharp knife to cut a few slits for air to escape, and bake for 30 – 35 minutes, until golden brown.

Note: For a discussion of the ins and outs of phyllo dough, see the baklava recipe on page 21 (for this recipe there is no need to clarify the butter).

Nothing and Like It

This is most often "what's for dinner?" in my house, and so is, in a sense, my signature dish. Adapted, of course, from *Caddyshack*, in which Judge Smails (Ted Knight) tells his obnoxious grandson (who is describing what he wants to eat), "you'll get nothing and like it!" (how anyone gets through a day without quoting *Caddyshack* is beyond me).

Every generation of my family has had its own version of this dish; my father was always serving "pink titty nipples." With my grandparents, it was "Kie bebis mit lukshen," which is Yiddish for cow shit with noodles (literally cow "beans" with noodles, but do not look for cow beans in the supermarket – they are found exclusively in the field, behind the cows…). I have always appreciated that, in all of the many meals I had with them, the kie bebis was always to be served with lukshen – as if one would never even consider serving kie bebis without lukshen; that would be gross.

Yield: Nothing.

Recommended Reading

Here are some good cookbooks, alphabetically by author.

The Tassajara Bread Book by Edward Espe Brown.
> This is essentially the zen of bread making, and a great place to start. *Tassajara Cooking* is also good (the basics of how to make everything vegetarian – rice, grains, beans, and – of course – vegetables…), and it's worth getting *The Tassajara Recipe Book* even if it's just to make the "Fresh Ginger Gingerbread" – *wow*.

Seitan and Beyond by Skye Michael Conroy.
> Vegan "meats" of every type. Try the meatballs (meatball parmigiana subs – *amazing*). My vegetarian "chicken," "gyro," and "sausage" recipes are all adapted from this excellent book.

Southern Italian Desserts by Rosetta Costantino.
> Some of the recipes are wildly complicated, and not all of them work out just so… Still, a great cookbook nonetheless, with quite a few excellent butter-less cookie recipes (in particular, check out the "Puglia and Basilicata" chapter), and some good advice for making cannoli.

Moosewood Cookbook by Mollie Katzen; a true classic.

Vegetarian Cooking for Everyone by Deborah Madison.
> A staple in our house – there are so many recipes we make from this book, and so many we have yet to try. Her "Saffron Noodle Cake" (known around here as "Spaghetti Pie") is a true family favorite (add 7/8 of a teaspoon of salt…). "Spiced Dried Fruits in Wine Syrup" is a real treat over tapioca pudding.

The Smitten Kitchen Cookbook and *Smitten Kitchen Every Day* by Deb Perelman.
> Deb can *cook*. Wow. You need these. Make the "Cheddar Buns" in the first book (they don't have to be for breakfast; warm the milk first), and the "Potatoes Anna" in the second. And everything else…

The New Book of Middle Eastern Food by Claudia Roden.
> I am mostly in love with the *Desserts, Pastries, and Sweetmeats* chapter, but there are plenty of great recipes in this book. Try the "Kaab el Ghzal" ("Gazelle Horns" – a nut filled pastry), and the "Stuffed Dates" (go overboard with the pistachios…).

The Essential Mediterranean Cookbook, Whitecap Books (no listed author).
> A treasure trove of good stuff (and an unimaginably ambitious undertaking – to cover not only the cuisines of Italy, France, and Spain, but also Greece, Turkey, North Africa, and the Middle East, all in one book). Check out the "Orange and Date Salad" – amazing.

Calculating Nutritional Information

I suppose I could just do it for you, for each recipe, but I'd rather show you how – it's not difficult. Of course, there are websites and applications that will do all of this, but there is a certain satisfaction that comes from doing it yourself. And it is undoubtedly more accurate – who knows what assumptions those websites and applications are making?

So, as an example, let's compute how many calories there are in a bialy (page 118). We will compute how many calories in an entire batch, and then divide by 18, since the recipe makes 18 bialys.

The dough is made up of water, yeast, salt, and bread flour. The water contributes no calories. According to the package, yeast has 390 calories per 100 grams, so

$$\frac{390}{100} \text{ calories per gram.}$$

The bialy recipe calls for 4 grams of yeast, so the yeast contributes

$$4\left(\frac{390}{100}\right) = 15.6 \text{ calories.}$$

(Calculators are permitted…) Like the water, the salt has no calories. The nutritional information on the bag of bread flour claims that there are 110 calories in 30 grams; since we use 1024 grams of bread flour, that is a total contribution of

$$1024\left(\frac{110}{30}\right) = 3754.7 \text{ calories}$$

(where 110/30 is the number of calories in a single gram, multiplied by 1024 since that is how many grams of flour in the recipe).

That takes care of the dough; there is also the filling to consider. A quick internet search indicates that a medium onion (which is what the recipe calls for) has 44 calories; this may not be the most accurate measurement (what is a *medium* onion?), but it's also a fairly minor contribution to the total amount, so good enough. I use a tablespoon of matzoh meal; the package declares that 1/2 cup has 100 calories. Since 1/2 cup is 8 tablespoons, this is

$$\frac{100}{8} = 12.5 \text{ calories per tablespoon,}$$

so (after multiplying by 1 for one tablespoon), 12.5 calories total from the matzoh meal. Finally, the poppy seeds, according to their packaging, have 45 calories per tablespoon. The recipe calls for "1 or 2 teaspoons;" if we go with 1 1/2 teaspoons, then that's half a tablespoon, so 45/2 = 22.5 calories.

Putting it all together, for the entire batch we have:

yeast:	15.6 calories
bread flour:	3754.7
onion:	44.0
matzoh meal:	12.5
poppy seeds:	22.5
Total:	3849.3 calories

So a batch of bialys has 3849.3 calories. Since there are 18 bialys in a batch, that means each bialy has 3849.3 / 18 = 213.85 calories, or about 214 calories.

The beauty of this technique is that it works exactly the same if you want to compute how much protein, or sodium, or folic acid, or vitamin B_{12} in a bialy – you just look up those values instead of calories for each of the ingredients. It also lets you use the nutritional information for the particular ingredients you're using – my yeast has 390 calories per 100 grams; yours might be slightly different. And of course you can apply it to any recipe, in this book or any other. Have fun…

Index

6-Strand Braid, **112**

African Peanut Soup, **178**
almonds
    in *Baklava*, 21
    in *Carrot Soup*, 176
    in *Chocolate Granola*, 66
    in *Granola*, 64
    in *Mandel Bread*, 34
    in *Modica*, 82
    in *Nut Balls*, 53
    in *Sicilian Almond Cookies*, 27
Angel Food Cake, **40**
asparagus
    in *Broccoli Strudel*, 188

Bagel Crackers (Hy's Amazing), **116**
Bagels, **113**
Baklava, **21**
Banana Chocolate Chip Scones, **104**
barley malt syrup
    in *Bagels*, 113
    in *Sunflower Bread*, 132
    in *Tahini Sandwich Cookies*, 33
beer
    in *Cheddar Ale Sauce*, 186
Bialys, **118**
Bing Cherry Pie, **8**
Black Tofu, **217**
blueberries
    in *Blueberry Muffins*, 93
    in *Blueberry Pancakes*, 70
Blueberry Muffins (Melissa's), **93**
Blueberry Pancakes, **70**
braid, 6-strand, 112
bread
    Bagels, 113
    Bialys, 118
    Breadsticks, 144
    Challah, 110
    Dinner or Burger Rolls, 124
    Flour Tortillas, 142
    French Bread Baguettes, 127
    Fruit, Nut, and Seed Bread, 134
    General Instructions, 108
    Khachapuri Rolls, 121
    Oat Bread, 136
    Pita Bread, 140
    Potato Bread, 138
    Sandwich Bread, 129
    Sunflower Bread, 132
Breadcrumbs, **146**
    in *Broccoli Strudel*, 188
    in *Macaroni and Cheese*, 208
    in *Modica*, 82
    in *Pasta with Roasted Cauliflower*, 213
Breadsticks (Crispy, Cheesy), **144**
broccoli
    in *Broccoli Strudel*, 188
    in *Pasta with Broccoli and Garlic*, 206
    in *Pasta with Crispy Chickpeas*, 205
    in *Vegetable Fried Rice*, 237
Broccoli Log, **188**
Broccoli Pockets, **188**
Broccoli Ring, **188**
Broccoli Strudel, **188**
Burger Rolls, **124**
buttermilk
    in *Banana Chocolate Chip Scones*, 104
    in *Blueberry Muffins*, 93
    in *Buttermilk Pancakes*, 70
    in *Buttermilk Waffles*, 71
    in *Corn Bread*, 98

in *Irish Soda Bread*, 100
in *Strawberry Muffins*, 92
Buttermilk Pancakes, **70**
Buttermilk Waffles, **71**

Caddyshack, 247
Caesar Salad, **74**
cake
    Angel Food Cake, 40
    Chocolate Cake, 46
    Orange Cake, 48
Calculating Nutritional Information, **250**
calzone, spinach, 215
Candied Cherries, **25**
Candied Nuts, **79**
carob powder
    in *Date Balls*, 52
    in *Tahini Sandwich Cookies*, 33
Carrot Soup (Simple But Excellent), **176**
carrots
    in *Carrot Soup*, 176
    in *Vegetable Fried Rice*, 237
Cashew Burgers, **192**
cashews
    in *Cashew Burgers*, 192
    in *Fake Chicken with Cashews*, 197
    in *Granola*, 64
cauliflower
    in *Pasta with Roasted Cauliflower*, 213
Challah, **110**
Cheddar Ale Sauce, **186**
Cheese:
    American grana
        in *"Dancing Heart" Pizza*, 158
        in *Potato Pizza*, 160
    asiago
        in *"Dancing Heart" Pizza*, 158
        in *Old Bay Pizza*, 162
        in *Potato Pizza*, 160
    cheddar
        in *Broccoli Strudel*, 188
        in *Cashew Burgers*, 192
        in *Cheddar Ale Sauce*, 186
        in *Macaroni and Cheese*, 208
        in *Mashed Potato Casserole*, 225
        in *Potato Cheese Soup*, 180
        in *Potato Pizza*, 160
        in *Vegetable Pot Pies*, 245
    feta
        in *Khachapuri Rolls*, 121
    gruyere
        in *Potato Pizza*, 160
    monterey jack
        in *Vegetarian Pastelón*, 226
    mozzarella
        in *New York Style Pizza*, 154
        in *Old Bay Pizza*, 162
        in *Potato Pizza*, 160
        in *Sicilian Pizza*, 156
        in *Spinach Calzone*, 215
    mozzarella, fresh
        in *Khachapuri Rolls*, 121
    paneer
        in *Saag Paneer*, 228
    pecorino romano
        in *Breadcrumbs*, 146
        in *Caesar Salad*, 74
        in *New York Style Pizza*, 154
        in *Pasta with Broccoli and Garlic*, 206
        in *Pasta with Crispy Chickpeas*, 205
        in *Pasta with Roasted Cauliflower*, 213
        in *Sicilian Pizza*, 156
        in *Spinach Calzone*, 215
        in *Spinach Ravioli*, 211
    provolone
        in *Old Bay Pizza*, 162
    ricotta
        in *Spinach Calzone*, 215
        in *Spinach Ravioli*, 211
    various
        in *Breadsticks*, 144
chicken, *see* Fake Chicken
chickpeas
    in *Pasta with Crispy Chickpeas*, 205
Chocolate Bread (Hy's Amazing), **42**
Chocolate Cake (The Best), **46**
Chocolate Chip Pancakes, **70**

chocolate chips
    in *Banana Chocolate Chip Scones*, 104
    in *Chocolate Cake*, 46
    in *Chocolate Chip Pancakes*, 70
    in *Pumpkin Chocolate Chip Muffins*, 96
Chocolate Granola, **66**
Chocolate Pudding Pie with a Walnut Crust, **16**
Cinnamon Buns, **44**
cocoa
    in *Chocolate Bread*, 42
    in *Chocolate Cake*, 46
    in *Chocolate Pudding*, 54
    in *Ice Cream Sandwiches*, 50
Cold Sesame Noodles, **202**
Common Ground restaurant, 33, 192
cookies
    Hermit Cookies, 30
    Lemon Raspberry Cookies, 28
    Sicilian Almond Cookies, 27
    Tahini Sandwich Cookies, 33
Corn Bread, **98**
Corn Muffins, **98**
crab
    in *Crab Cakes*, 200
Crab Cakes (Bill's), **200**
Creole Seasoning, **232**
Cucumber Yogurt Sauce, **84**
cucumbers
    in *Cucumber Yogurt Sauce*, 84
    in *Vietnamese Cucumber Salad*, 78

D'Orazio, Valeria, 48
"Dancing Heart" Pizza, **158**
Date Balls, **52**
Date Nut Bread, **102**
dates
    in *Date Balls*, 52
    in *Date Nut Bread*, 102
Dennis, Elmer L., 7
Dinner Rolls, **124**
Drop Biscuits, **90**
Dutch Baby Pancake, **72**

Fake Chicken, **199**
Fake Chicken with Cashews, **197**
filo dough, *see* phyllo dough
Flour Tortillas, **142**
Focaccia, **168**
Focaccia with Leeks, **170**
Fox, Jackie, 82
French Bread Baguettes, **127**
Fruit, Nut, and Seed Bread, **134**

Garcia, Jerry, 56
Garlic Pasta, **207**
General Instructions, **108**
General Notes, **148**
Gingerbread Pancakes, **70**
Ginsberg
    Becky, 38, 223, 243
    Butchie, 34
    Marty, 34, 38
Granola, **64**
    Chocolate Granola, 66
Grateful Dead, 56
Grilled Pizza, **166**
Gyro Pockets (Vegetarian), **194**

Half and Half Pie Crust, **6**
Herbed Flatbread, **173**
Hermit Cookies, **30**

Ice Cream Sandwiches, **50**
Indian Pudding, **56**
Irish Soda Bread (Aunt Sue's), **100**

Jewish foods
    Bagels, 113
    Bialys, 118
    Challah, 110
    Kie bebis, 247
    Mandel Bread, 34
    Potatonik, 223
    Rugelach, 38
    Sour Garlic Pickles, 76
    Varenikas, 243

Kane, Bill, 166, 200

Khachapuri Rolls, **121**

leeks
    in *Focaccia with Leeks*, 170

leftover rice
    in *Cashew Burgers*, 192
    in *Vegetable Fried Rice*, 237

Lemon Bars, **37**
Lemon Raspberry Cookies, **28**

lentils
    in *Mujadara*, 233

Macaroni and Cheese, **208**
Macaroni and Cheese Pizza, **159**
malted barley, *see* barley malt syrup
Mandel Bread (Ginsberg's), **34**
Marmalade, **80**
Mashed Potato Casserole, **225**

millet
    in *Sandwich Bread*, 129

Mingrelian khachapuri, 121
Mint Julep, **86**
Modica, **82**

molasses
    in *Hermit Cookies*, 30
    in *Indian Pudding*, 56
    in *Oat Bread*, 136
    in *Pumpkin Pie*, 12

muffins
    Blueberry Muffins, 93
    Pumpkin Chocolate Chip Muffins, 96
    Strawberry Muffins, 92

Mujadara, **233**
Multigrain Waffles, **71**

New York Style Pizza, **154**
Nothing and Like It, **247**
Nut Balls, **53**
nutritional information, 250

nutritional yeast
    in *Garlic Pasta*, 207
    in *Surfer Spread*, 85

Oat Bread, **136**
oats
    in *Chocolate Granola*, 66
    in *Granola*, 64
    in *Oat Bread*, 136
    in *Sandwich Bread*, 129
    in *Tahini Sandwich Cookies*, 33

Old Bay Pizza, **162**
Orange Cake (Valeria's Italian), **48**
Ottolenghi, 217

Pancakes, **69**
    Blueberry Pancakes, 70
    Buttermilk Pancakes, 70
    Chocolate Chip Pancakes, 70
    Gingerbread Pancakes, 70
    Pecan Pancakes, 70

pasta
    Cold Sesame Noodles, 202
    Garlic Pasta, 207
    Macaroni and Cheese, 208
    Pasta with Broccoli and Garlic, 206
    Pasta with Crispy Chickpeas, 205
    Pasta with Roasted Cauliflower, 213
    Spinach Ravioli, 211

Pasta with Broccoli and Garlic, **206**
Pasta with Crispy Chickpeas, **205**
Pasta with Roasted Cauliflower, **213**

pastry
    Baklava, 21
    Rugelach, 38

Peach Pie, **10**

peanut butter
    in *African Peanut Soup*, 178
    in *Cold Sesame Noodles*, 202
    in *Peanut Sauce*, 83
    in *Tahini Sandwich Cookies*, 33

Peanut Sauce, **83**
Pecan Pancakes, **70**
Pecan Pie, **14**
Pecan Waffles, **71**

pecans
    in *Pecan Pancakes*, 70
    in *Pecan Pie*, 14
    in *Pecan Waffles*, 71

phyllo dough

in *Baklava*, 21
in *Broccoli Strudel*, 188
in *Vegetable Pot Pies*, 245
pickles, sour garlic, 76
pie
  Bing Cherry Pie, 8
  Chocolate Pudding Pie with a Walnut Crust, 16
  Peach Pie, 10
  Pecan Pie, 14
  Pumpkin Pie, 12
pistachios
  in *Baklava*, 21
  in *Saffron Rice Pilaf*, 240
Pita Bread, **140**
pizza
  General Notes, 148
  Grilled Pizza, 166
  Macaroni and Cheese Pizza, 159
  New York Style Pizza, 154
  Old Bay Pizza, 162
  Potato Pizza, 160
  Scallion Pancake Pizza, 164
  Sicilian Pizza, 156
  "Dancing Heart" Pizza, 158
Pizza Dough, **151**
Pizza Sauce, **153**
plantains
  in *Vegetarian Pastelón*, 226
Potato Bread, **138**
Potato Cheese Soup, **180**
Potato Pizza, **160**
potatoes
  in *Focaccia with Leeks*, 170
  in *Mashed Potato Casserole*, 225
  in *Potato Bread*, 138
  in *Potato Cheese Soup*, 180
  in *Potato Pizza*, 160
  in *Potatonik*, 223
  in *Seafood Soup*, 182
  in *Varenikas*, 243
Potatonik (Becky's), **223**
protein crumbles
  in *Turkish Pizza*, 235
  in *Vegetarian Pastelón*, 226
pudding
  Indian Pudding, 56
  Rice Pudding, 58
  Tapioca Pudding, 60
  Vanilla or Chocolate Pudding, 54
pumpkin
  in *Pumpkin Chocolate Chip Muffins*, 96
  in *Pumpkin Pie*, 12
Pumpkin Chocolate Chip Muffins, **96**
Pumpkin Pie, **12**
pumpkin seeds
  in *Fruit, Nut, and Seed Bread*, 134
  in *Granola*, 64
raisins
  in *Date Balls*, 52
  in *Fruit, Nut, and Seed Bread*, 134
  in *Hermit Cookies*, 30
  in *Irish Soda Bread*, 100
  in *Mandel Bread*, 34
  in *Rice Pudding*, 58
  in *Rugelach*, 38
  in *Saffron Rice Pilaf*, 240
raspberry jam, 98
  in *Lemon Raspberry Cookies*, 28
Recommended Reading, **249**
rice
  in *Cashew Burgers*, 192
  in *Mujadara*, 233
  in *Rice Pudding*, 58
  in *Saffron Rice Pilaf*, 240
  in *Vegetable Fried Rice*, 237
Rice Pudding, **58**
Roasted Tofu, **220**
rolls, 124
Rugelach, **38**

Saag Paneer, **228**
saffron
  in *Saffron Rice Pilaf*, 240
Saffron Rice Pilaf, **240**
salad

  Caesar Salad, 74
  Vietnamese Cucumber Salad, 78
salmon
  in *Seafood Soup*, 182
Sandwich Bread (Hy's Best), **129**
sauce
  Cucumber Yogurt Sauce, 84
  Tahini Yogurt Sauce, 84
Scallion Pancake Pizza, **164**
Scallion Pancakes, **165**
scallops
  in *Seafood Soup*, 182
scones, banana chocolate chip, 104
seafood
  Crab Cakes, 200
  Old Bay Pizza, 162
  Seafood Soup, 182
  Shrimp Etouffee, 231
Seafood Soup, **182**
shrimp
  in *Old Bay Pizza*, 162
  in *Seafood Soup*, 182
  in *Shrimp Etouffee*, 231
Shrimp Etouffee, **231**
Shrimp Stock, **232**
Sicilian Almond Cookies, **27**
Sicilian Pizza, **156**
Sides, Melissa, 93
soup
  African Peanut Soup, 178
  Carrot Soup, 176
  Potato Cheese Soup, 180
  Seafood Soup, 182
Sour Garlic Pickles, **76**
Spanik, Sue, 100
spinach
  in *Saag Paneer*, 228
  in *Spinach Ravioli*, 211
Spinach Calzone, **215**
Spinach Ravioli, **211**
Strawberry Muffins, **92**
sun-dried tomatoes, *see* tomatoes, sun-dried
Sunflower Bread, **132**

sunflower seeds
  in *Fruit, Nut, and Seed Bread*, 134
  in *Granola*, 64
  in *Sunflower Bread*, 132
  in *Tahini Sandwich Cookies*, 33
Surfer Spread, **85**

tahini
  in *Cold Sesame Noodles*, 202
  in *Tahini Sandwich Cookies*, 33
  in *Tahini Yogurt Sauce*, 84
Tahini Sandwich Cookies, **33**
Tahini Yogurt Sauce, **84**
Tapioca Pudding, **60**
tofu
  in *Black Tofu*, 218
  in *Fake Chicken*, 199
  in *Roasted Tofu*, 220
  in *Surfer Spread*, 85
tomatoes, sun-dried
  in *Pasta with Crispy Chickpeas*, 205
  in *Surfer Spread*, 85
Turkish Pizza, **235**
tzatziki, 84

udon noodles
  in *Cold Sesame Noodles*, 202

Vanilla or Chocolate Pudding, **54**
Varenikas (Becky's), **243**
Vegetable Fried Rice, **237**
Vegetable Pot Pies, **245**
Vegetable Stock, **184**
Vegetarian "meats"
  Fake Chicken, 199
  Gyro Pockets, 194
  Vegetarian Sausage, 155
Vegetarian Pastelón, **226**
Vegetarian Sausage, **155**
Vietnamese Cucumber Salad, **78**
vital wheat gluten
  in *Fake Chicken*, 199
  in *Gyro Pockets*, 194
  in *Vegetarian Sausage*, 155

Waffles, **71**
- *Buttermilk Waffles*, 71
- *Multigrain Waffles*, 71
- *Pecan Waffles*, 71

walnuts
- in *Baklava*, 21
- in *Cashew Burgers*, 192
- in *Chocolate Pudding Pie with a Walnut Crust*, 16
- in *Fruit, Nut, and Seed Bread*, 134
- in *Hermit Cookies*, 30
- in *Rugelach*, 38

yogurt
- in *Cucumber Yogurt Sauce*, 84
- in *Khachapuri Rolls*, 121
- in *Saag Paneer*, 228
- in *Tahini Yogurt Sauce*, 84
- in *Turkish Pizza*, 235

Zucker, Gil, 34

About the Author

Me. (It's customary to pretend that someone else wrote this part, but I can't bring myself to willfully deceive you.) I live in Massachusetts with Anne, Evan, and Daisy (see the dedication), and teach mathematics at Worcester State University. If you've gotten this far, then you already know I have something of a sweet tooth, am into bread and pizza, don't mind paper plates, and I never iron. You may also have gleaned that I do a little pottery on the side (I do). In the past (and hopefully the near future) I've been a painter; I also call myself a musician (search for "Hy's Home Recordings" on YouTube if you're so inclined), and I'm certainly a serious Deadhead. Very concerned about climate change, the probable imminent collapse of civilization, and the possible extinction of our very unusual and exasperating species… I should clearly shut up now, so I will. I hope you liked the book.

Made in the USA
Middletown, DE
11 December 2020